SNOW WHITE
AND
THE SEVEN DWARFS

"IN THE MEASURE TO ENSUE,
LADY, MAY I DANCE WITH YOU?"

SNOW WHITE
AND
THE SEVEN DWARFS

*A Fairy Tale Play Based on the
Story of the Brothers Grimm*

BY

JESSIE BRAHAM WHITE

WITH MUSIC BY
EDMOND RICKETT

AND NUMEROUS ILLUSTRATIONS BY
CHARLES B. FALLS

NEW YORK
DODD, MEAD & COMPANY
1913

Copyright, 1912
BY WINTHROP AMES

All acting rights strictly reserved

SNOW WHITE
AND
THE SEVEN DWARFS

MUSIC

ILLUSTRATIONS

The Persons of the Play

PRINCESS SNOW WHITE

QUEEN BRANGOMAR

ROSALYS   CHRISTABEL
AMELOTTE   ASTOLAINE   *Maids of Honor*
ERMENGARDE   URSULA   *to Snow White*
GUINIVERE   LINNETTE

SIR DANDIPRAT BOMBAS, *the Court Chamberlain*

BERTHOLD, *the Chief Huntsman*

PRINCE FLORIMOND *of Calydon*

VALENTINE
VIVIAN   *Pages to the Prince*

BLICK   PLICK
FLICK   WHICK
GLICK   QUEE   *The Seven Dwarfs*
SNICK

WITCH HOX

FIDDLE, *her Cat*

DUKES, DUCHESSES and FLUNKIES.

Scene
I

THE THRONE ROOM IN
QUEEN BRANGOMAR'S PALACE

*The Throne Room is a fine apartment, hung with
blue damask embroidered with silver peacocks—
birds of which* QUEEN BRANGOMAR *is very fond.
At the back wide steps lead to a terrace of white
marble. Beyond shines the blue sea. On one
side stands the great throne, inlaid with coloured
mosaics. Opposite is an entrance leading to the
other rooms of the palace.*

When the Play begins, seven of the MAIDS OF HON-
OUR TO PRINCESS SNOW WHITE *are playing a
game with coloured balls. They are little girls
about twelve years old, and their names are* ROS-
ALYS, AMELOTTE, ERMENGARDE, GUINIVERE,
CHRISTABEL, URSULA *and* LINNETTE. *As they
play they sing:*

SNOW WHITE

Game of Ball

Music by
Edmond Rickett. Op.25

Allegretto (♩ = 104)

High and low, High and low, Round - a - bout and 'cross they go. Blue and green, gold and white, Toss them true and hold them tight.

SCENE I

GAME OF BALL SONG.

MAIDS OF HONOUR.

 High and low,
 High and low,
Round about and 'cross they go.
 Blue and green,
 Gold and white,
Toss them true and hold them tight.
 Miss a ball,
 Let it fall,
Make the least mistake at all;
 One, two, three,
 Out goes she!
One, two, three, *and* out goes she!
 [*Just here* ROSALYS *does miss, and the others rush to* "*tag*" *her, crying,* "Rosalys is out!" "Rosalys is out!"

ROSALYS. I don't care. It's not an interesting game anyway!

CHRISTABEL. Play again?

ERMENGARDE. One game.

GUINIVERE. I will.

SCENE I

[*But just as they are about to begin again,*
SIR DANDIPRAT BOMBAS, *the Court
Chamberlain, appears on the terrace.
He is a fat, puffy little man, with an
enormous wig and a great sense of his
own importance.*

SIR DANDIPRAT. Ah, young ladies . . . What?
Playing in the Throne Room? Tut, tut! Tut,
tut!

MAIDS OF HONOUR. Oh, please don't tell.
Don't tell the Queen.
We didn't break any-
thing.

SIR DANDIPRAT. No,
on the whole I won't tell
her Majesty. She *might*
blame me. As I was go-
ing to say, I have an im-
portant announcement to
make. Since Lady Cecily
was sent home with the mumps your usual number,
eight, has been reduced to seven. Am I right?

[5]

One from eight leaves seven I think? [*He tries to do the sum on his fingers.*]

ROSALYS. Yes, it is seven.

SIR DANDIPRAT. I *am* right. Her Majesty the Queen wishes your number kept complete, so I have brought another young lady to take the vacant place. [*He leads on little* LADY ASTOLAINE *and presents her:*] The Lady Astolaine. These are the Maids of Honour to the Princess Snow White.

[LADY ASTOLAINE *curtsies to the* MAIDS OF
HONOUR *and they in turn curtsey to her.*
SIR DANDIPRAT *goes on*

You must teach Lady Astolaine all she ought to know as a Maid of Honour. You'd better teach her your gavotte first; you may have to dance it almost immediately. [*And the little man dances a few steps, puffing out the tune meantime:*] "Tum, tum, tum, ti; dum, tum, tum, ti! And how to make a proper curtsey—so. [*And he tries to make one.*] And how to retire backwards gracefully—so! [*But as he retires backwards he stumbles against the terrace steps, and falls flat on his*

[6]

back. He is so embarrassed by this mishap that he scrambles out of the room as fast as he can, puffing:] Gracefully, young ladies! Gracefully! Gracefully! [*till he is out of sight*].

ASTOLAINE. [*Laughing.*] Who's that old thing?

ROSALYS. [*Mimicking* SIR DANDIPRAT'S *voice and strut.*] That's Sir Dandiprat Bombas, Court Chamberlain to the Queen.

CHRISTABEL. He gives us our "instructions."

ERMENGARDE. But we don't mind *him.*

ASTOLAINE. Do you have good times here?

ROSALYS. Splendid; except [*confidentially*] when the Queen is especially cross.

CHRISTABEL. And then, oh me! we have to be careful!

ASTOLAINE. I don't think I shall like the Queen!

MAIDS OF HONOUR. [*Hastily.*] Ssh!

[7]

ASTOLAINE. Why, ssh?

ROSALYS. [*Whispering.*] Never say anything uncomplimentary about the Queen!

MAIDS OF HONOUR. [*Loudly, intending to be overheard.*] We all *adore* the Queen! [*But they shake their heads, and make little faces to show* ASTOLAINE *that they don't mean it.*]

ASTOLAINE. [*Whispering.*] I shall *hate* the Queen!

MAIDS OF HONOUR. [*Also whispering.*] *We* all do!

ASTOLAINE. But I'm to be Maid of Honour to the Princess Snow White, so I'll take my orders from her.

ROSALYS. Oh, Snow White never gives orders.

ASTOLAINE. I shall like *her*. When shall I see her?

CHRISTABEL. Sometimes, every day; and then again not for ever so long. It just depends on the Queen's temper.

SIR DANDIPRAT BOMBAS, THE COURT CHAMBERLAIN, APPEARS
ON THE TERRACE

ERMENGARDE. And how much Snow White has to do.

ASTOLAINE. I thought a Princess never had anything to do.

CHRISTABEL. [*Confidentially.*] Well, you see, Snow White isn't exactly a regular Princess.

ROSALYS. Why, Christabel! Of course she's a regular Princess, but . . .

ASTOLAINE. But what? [*Wonderingly.*] You don't hate Snow White too?

MAIDS OF HONOUR. [*In indignant chorus.*] Hate Snow White! The idea! She's the dearest! Loveliest! Kindest! We just adore her!

ROSALYS. [*To the others.*] Oh, do you think we could get Snow White to come and see Astolaine now, while we're all alone?

CHRISTABEL. Oh, let's try! [*And all the little*

MAIDS *hop up and down and clap their hands with glee at the idea.*]

ROSALYS. Where is she?

CHRISTABEL. Kitchen, I think. She said she had to bake bread first and cookies afterward.

ROSALYS. Bread is important, but cookies aren't. Anyway it can't do any harm to ask her.

AMELOTTE. I'll go! I'll go! [*And off she darts to the kitchen.*]

ASTOLAINE. [*Wonderingly.*] But what is the Princess doing in the kitchen?

ROSALYS. Of course you don't understand about Snow White yet. It's a court secret. [*To the others.*] But I think we ought to tell her right away, don't you? before she sees Snow White, or she might think . . .
> [*They evidently agree, for they all rush at ASTOLAINE and begin to speak at once.*

MAIDS OF HONOUR. I'll tell her! No, let me, I

know! Snow White was born . . . This Queen isn't her real mother. It's like a fairy-tale!

ASTOLAINE. [*Stopping her ears.*] I can't *possibly* understand if you all talk at once. [*But each little* MAID, *thinking that the others will stop, again begins to tell* SNOW WHITE's *story, so that the confusion is worse than before.* ASTOLAINE *has to hold her ears a second time.*] That's worse! There's only one fair way to decide. I'll "count out," and the one that's out shall tell.

ROSALYS. Hm! I suppose that's fair,—only I should tell it so much the best.

CHRISTABEL. [*To* ASTOLAINE.] Well then, you count.

> [*So* ASTOLAINE *sings the "Counting-out Song," counting as she sings.*

SNOW WHITE

Counting-out Song

Music by
Edmond Rickett. Op. 25

In-try, min-try, cut-ty corn, Ap-ple seed and

ap-ple thorn, Wire, briar, limb-er lock, Five grey geese in a flock;

Ee-ny, mee-ny, mo-na, mi, Bass-a-lo-na, bo-na, stri,

One, two, three, Out goes she; Out goes she!

SCENE I

"Intry, mintry, cutry, corn,
"Apple seed and apple thorn;
"Wire, briar, limber, lock,
"Five grey geese in a flock.
"Eeny, meeny, mona, mi,
"Bassalona, bona stri.
   "One, two, three,
   "Out goes she!
   "Out—goes—she!"

      [*The last count falls on* ROSALYS.

MAIDS OF HONOUR. [*Regretfully.*] Oh, it's Rosalys!

ROSALYS. I was so afraid it wouldn't be me. Come over here where we can talk quietly. [*She runs to the throne and climbs into the big seat. The others cuddle close beside her.*] Now, nobody must interrupt, except by 'spress permission. Button mouths! First, Queen Brangomar isn't Snow White's real mother.

ASTOLAINE. Oh, I know *that!*

[13]

CHRISTABEL. But my father says that her real father and mother were the best King and Queen . . .

ROSALYS. [*Glaring at* CHRISTABEL.] What about interrupting?

CHRISTABEL. I forgot. 'Scuse me! [*And she "buttons" her mouth again.*]

SCENE I

The Story of Snow-white

Music by
Edmond Rickett. Op.25

Rosalys. [*Continuing.*] One day in winter before Snow White was born, her real mother was sitting by the window embroidering at an ebony frame. And she pricked her finger, so she opened the window and shook the drop of blood on the snow outside. And it looked so beautiful that she said, "Oh, how I wish I had a little daughter with hair as black as ebony, skin as white as snow, and lips as red as blood. She'd never had a baby before; but a little while after a baby daughter was born with . . .

Maids of Honour. [*Chanting impressively.*] Hair as black as ebony, skin as white as snow, and lips as red as blood.

Astolaine. So *that's* why they named her Snow White.

Rosalys. But then Snow White's mother died; and I suppose the King thought there ought to be *somebody* to mind the baby, for he married Queen Brangomar—she's Queen now.

Astolaine. Oh, I see!

ROSALYS. As long as the King lived, Queen Brangomar was as sweet as sugar to Snow White.

CHRISTABEL. [*Interrupting in a whisper.*] I am glad she was ever nice to somebody.

ROSALYS. But after he died, then— [*She pauses impressively.*]

ASTOLAINE. Then . . . what?

ROSALYS. Then—she grew aw-fully jealous of Snow White.

ASTOLAINE. Not really?

ERMENGARDE. Of course everybody loved the Princess best.

CHRISTABEL. And Brangomar really is the hor-ridest woman!

ROSALYS. Ssh! First she pretended that Snow White might grow up vain, so she took away all her princessy clothes and made her wear old, rag-bag-gety things.

CHRISTABEL. Then she pretended that she might

grow up lazy, so she made her sweep and dust the Palace.

ROSALYS. And now Snow White is really almost like a kitchen-maid, and sleeps in a little closet under the stairs where we keep the umbrellas and overshoes.

ASTOLAINE. [*Springing up.*] I think it's outrageous! Why does Princess Snow White stand it? I wouldn't!

MAIDS OF HONOUR. [*Apprehensively.*] Oh, ssh!

ASTOLAINE. Why "ssh"? I never heard anything so "sshy" as this Palace.

ROSALYS. [*Whispering.*] But what can she do? The Queen . . .

ASTOLAINE. I don't want to hear any more about that hateful Queen.

ROSALYS. But you must. It isn't safe that you shouldn't. We'll *have* to tell her. [*To* CHRISTA-BEL.] *You* tell.

CHRISTABEL. No, you. It makes me feel all creepy.

ROSALYS. [*To* ERMENGARDE.] Well, *you!*

ERMENGARDE. No! You were counted out.

ASTOLAINE. Well, please somebody!

ROSALYS. Oh, dear! [*She goes on in a hushed whisper.*] The reason it's not safe to do or say anything against the Queen is—that she might *magic* you!

ASTOLAINE. What do you mean?

ROSALYS. Enchant you, bewitch you;—do some terrible magic thing to you!

ASTOLAINE. You don't mean that she's a . . . Witch? [*The others nod silently, and snuggle closer together.*]

ROSALYS. If she isn't a Witch herself she is friends with one. You see she must really be very old.

CHRISTABEL. She's thirty if she's a minute!

ROSALYS. And she's still the most beautiful woman in the Seven Kingdoms.

CHRISTABEL. And once a chamber-maid found a broom-stick, the kind that witches ride on, in her bed-room.

ROSALYS. So you see if you did anything against her she might magic you, and turn you into a pig.

ERMENGARDE. Or a toad.

ROSALYS. Or a caterpillar.

CHRISTABEL. Or something worse.

ASTOLAINE. There isn't anything worse than a caterpillar! Oh, I want to go home! I am afraid! [*And she bursts into tears. The others gather about to comfort her.*]

MAIDS OF HONOUR. Please, Astolaine, there's really nothing to be afraid of. It's all right, honestly. The Queen hardly ever notices us! And we all want you to stay, for we like you ever so much.

ROSALYS. [*In despair.*] Oh, if Snow White

would only come now! Then she wouldn't want to go home.

> [*Just at this moment* AMELOTTE *reappears in the doorway.*]

AMELOTTE. Princess Snow White says she'll come if nobody's here.

GUINIVERE. There isn't anybody.

AMELOTTE. She'll come! She'll come! She's right here! [*And she darts out of sight again.*]

ROSALYS. Oh, she's coming! Snow White's coming! Now you'll see!

> [*In joyous excitement the* MAIDS OF HONOUR *join hands and dance a "ring-around," and then wind up into a little squirming knot, hugging each other and dancing up and down.*]

AMELOTTE. [*Re-entering, announces.*] The Princess Snow White!

> [*Instantly the* MAIDS OF HONOUR *separate and kneel to receive their little Princess.*]

[SNOW WHITE *appears in the doorway.
She is dressed in a frock of ragged black,
and she has on neither shoes nor stockings. Nevertheless she has the air of a
little Princess.*

SNOW WHITE. Is this my new playmate, Lady
Astolaine? I hope you'll like me.

ASTOLAINE. [*Kissing the hand which* SNOW
WHITE *holds out to her.*] I love you already, dear
Princess.

[*Like a little flight of birds the* MAIDS OF
HONOUR *run to surround* SNOW WHITE.

MAIDS OF HONOUR. We all love you, dear Princess!

SNOW WHITE. [*Laughing down at them.*]
And I love you, all of you! But did you want anything particular? I've left hundreds of cookies in
my oven.

ROSALYS. Can't you stay just a moment and
teach Astolaine our gavotte? Sir Dandiprat said

[22]

that she must learn it at once; and you dance so much the best.

SNOW WHITE.   Do you think I have time?

MAIDS OF HONOUR.   Oh yes, yes!

ROSALYS.   [*Running out onto the terrace.*]   I'll watch, and tell if anybody's coming.

SNOW WHITE.   [*To* ASTOLAINE.]   You'd better be my partner.   It's very simple.

> [*The* MAIDS OF HONOUR *take positions for their Dance, and as* SNOW WHITE *teaches* ASTOLAINE *the steps they sing:*

SNOW WHITE

Maids of Honor Dance

Music by
Edmond Rickett. Op. 25

Turn to me and curt-sey low; One, two, three; One, two, three; Turn a - way and point your toe; One and two and three. Turn a - gain, and hand in hand, Hand in

SCENE I

hand,— Hand in— hand;— Turn your part-ner where you stand,—

One and two and three.— One and two and three.—

Fine

Più mosso (♩= 160)

SNOW WHITE

SCENE I

SNOW WHITE.

Turn to me and curtsey low.

THE MAIDS.

One, two, three,
One, two, three

SNOW WHITE.

Turn away and point your toe.

THE MAIDS.

One and two and three.

SNOW WHITE.

Turn again and hand in hand,

THE MAIDS.

Hand in hand,
Hand in hand

SNOW WHITE.

Turn your partner where you stand.

THE MAIDS.

One and two and three.
One and two . . .

[27]

[*But just here* ROSALYS *comes running in from the terrace.*

ROSALYS. Ssh! Old Dandiprat's coming!

SNOW WHITE. Oh dear, I must run . . .

ROSALYS. [*Catching her.*] No, don't! He won't stay a minute. Hide behind the throne till he's gone.

MAIDS OF HONOUR. Yes, yes. Quickly! Behind the throne! [SNOW WHITE *runs behind the throne, and the* MAIDS OF HONOUR *spread themselves out before it so that she is quite hidden. But they are not a moment too soon, for* SIR DANDIPRAT *waddles in from the terrace, followed by two solemn* FLUNKIES *in gorgeous liveries.*]

SIR DANDIPRAT. Ah, young ladies! I am fortunate to have found you all together. I have a most important announcement to make. I composed it myself. [*He unrolls an imposing parchment, and reads.*] "Whereas, our gracious Queen has been

[28]

informed that his Highness, Prince Florimond, heir to the Kingdom of Calydon, will call upon her Majesty this afternoon to deliver an important letter from his royal father, I have arranged the following reception. At four-fifteen precisely this Proclamation will be read." [*He consults his watch.*] Dear me! Five minutes late already! I shall have to alter it. [*And with a sigh he makes the correction with a gold pencil.*] "At four-*twenty* precisely this Proclamation will be read. At four-thirty Prince Florimond will arrive, and be shown at once to the throne-room by—ahem!—myself. The Maids of Honour will dance their gavotte to amuse his Highness until the Queen is announced, when they will immediately retire. By order of me, Sir Dandiprat Bombas, Court Chamberlain.

"Signed, Yours very truly,

"Sir Dandiprat Bombas."

"P. S. Her Majesty the Queen regrets that, owing to her duties in the kitchen, Princess Snow White will be unable to attend." You understand, young ladies?

ROSALYS. Perfectly, Sir Dandiprat.

SIR DANDIPRAT. You have eight minutes and thirty-one seconds to prepare. [*And he trips busily away again, followed by the* FLUNKIES.]

ASTOLAINE. Gracious! I can't possibly learn that dance in eight minutes and thirty-one seconds!

CHRISTABEL. And we *must* dance in pairs!

ERMENGARDE. What *shall* we do?

ROSALYS. [*Calling to* SNOW WHITE *who is still hidden behind the throne.*] Princess Snow White, what *shall* we do?
[*There is no answer.*]

ASTOLAINE. It's all right, Princess. Sir Dandiprat has gone.
    [*Still there is no answer; and puzzled, the little* MAIDS *call, one after another:*

ROSALYS. Princess Snow White!

CHRISTABEL. Princess Snow White!

GUINIVERE. Princess Snow White!

[30]

SCENE I

[*Still no answer.* ROSALYS *runs behind the throne.*

ROSALYS. Oh, she's crying! Oh, dear Princess!
[*They all run to* SNOW WHITE, *and find her hiding her face and sobbing silently.*

MAIDS OF HONOUR. [*Surrounding and embracing her.*] Oh, what's the matter? Please don't cry! We can't bear to see you unhappy! If you cry we shall cry, too!

SNOW WHITE. I didn't mean to cry. I won't! A princess should never cry. [*She smiles resolutely, though her eyes are full of tears.*] There! But I did so want to see Prince Florimond again. He sends me a valentine every year; and long ago, when his father came to visit mine, we were wheeled about in the same baby-carriage. He must be grown up now.

ASTOLAINE. I think it's an outrageous shame!

SNOW WHITE. But what can I do? You heard. [*Quoting.*] "P. S. Her Majesty regrets that the Princess will be unable to attend."

[31]

ASTOLAINE. If I were a princess I'd do what I chose, and if the Queen didn't like it I'd . . .

MAIDS OF HONOUR. [*Apprehensively.*] Astolaine! Hush!

ASTOLAINE. I'm tired of hushing.

SNOW WHITE. She's right! I am a king's daughter after all; and if I am always meek and do just what I'm told I'll stay in that hateful kitchen all my life. Oh! *wouldn't* I like to march right in before everybody and say, "Prince Florimond, I'm your cousin Snow White. I apologise for my frock, but it's all I have; and I can't let you kiss my hand because it's all covered with flour. But I did want to see you again, after riding with you in a baby-carriage when you were two and I was a half—and I have! Good-bye!" And then I'd march back to my kitchen.

MAIDS OF HONOUR. Oh, please, *please* don't, dear Princess!

ROSALYS. The Queen would be so angry she might even . . .

Lo! through a smoking circle in the floor, Witch Hex
does appear

ASTOLAINE. [*Struck with an idea.*] Wait! The Queen won't be here when we dance for the Prince?

ROSALYS. No. Why?

ASTOLAINE. Then why can't the Princess dance in my place? She could wear my veil over her face, and I'd say afterward that I had—oh, measles or something else spotty.

CHRISTABEL. [*In delight.*] Oh, Astolaine! [*She runs to hug her for the suggestion.*]

SNOW WHITE. Oh dear! I wish it were possible,—but my frock!

ROSALYS. Why can't we *all* lend her something?

CHRISTABEL. Why not? We have on heaps more than we need.

ROSALYS. She could have my over-skirt. [*She pulls it up to show an under-skirt almost as elaborate.*]

CHRISTABEL. And my "watteau."

AMELOTTE. And my lace jacket.

ERMENGARDE. And my cap and pearls.

ROSALYS. We could dress her perfectly! [*And they all hop up and down with little squeaks of delight.*]

ASTOLAINE. Will you do it, Princess? Oh, will you?

SNOW WHITE. You darlings! I suppose I oughtn't—but I will!

> [*And she runs behind the throne to dress, with* GUINIVERE *to help her. The other little* MAIDS *unpin and unhook and twist and turn to reach hard buttons at a great rate, as you can judge from the things they say.*

MAIDS OF HONOUR. Here's my veil! Oh, she doesn't want a veil first; help me with this skirt. I can't unhook me! These pearls just *won't* untangle! Please come and unpin this. No, me first! I won't go to either if you don't decide! She's ready for the skirt now. You unhook while

I squeeze. Now! one, two, three! There isn't
room for all our fingers on one little hook! Here's
the jacket!

> [*And now they're all behind the throne
> helping* SNOW WHITE *on with the new
> things, except poor* CHRISTABEL, *who is
> left writhing to reach a pin at the back
> of her neck.*]

CHRISTABEL. I think you're just mean! I know
it will prick! It did! Well, anyway, I know
where it is now. [*And with an enormous twist, she
succeeds in unfastening her "watteau."*]

ROSALYS. [*Dancing out, waving* SNOW
WHITE'S *black frock.*] Here's her little black
dress. What shall I do with it?

ASTOLAINE. [*Following.*] Oh, put it anywhere!

ROSALYS. But where *is* anywhere?

ASTOLAINE. Here, stuff it under this cushion on
the throne. [*She does so.*] They'll never find it

there. *Won't* it be a joke when the Queen sits on it?

ROSALYS. Oh, why did you say that? Now, I shall just giggle and giggle and giggle! [*And they run behind the throne again.*]

> [SNOW WHITE *is almost dressed now; and the little* MAIDS, *one after another, tip-toe away from the throne, whispering:*

CHRISTABEL.
Oh, she looks like a bride, and she's perfectly sweet.

ERMENGARDE.
All silver and white from her head to her feet.

ROSALYS.
Her lips red as blood, and her hair black as night!

ASTOLAINE.
She's lovely, she's lovely, our Princess Snow White.

> [*They stand waiting for her. There is a moment's pause, and then* ROSALYS *calls:*

ROSALYS. Aren't you coming, Princess?

[36]

SNOW WHITE. [*From behind the throne.*]
Just a moment, till I shake out my hair. There!
> [*She steps into sight. The* MAIDS *sink
> down in involuntary curtsies at the sight
> of her.*

CHRISTABEL. She is lovelier than apple blossoms.

ASTOLAINE. Lovelier than anybody I ever saw.

ROSALYS. [*In a hushed voice.*] More beautiful than the Queen!

CHRISTABEL. [*Whispering.*] The Queen must never see her like this.

GUINIVERE. Never!

SNOW WHITE. [*Who has been putting the last touches to her dress,—suddenly.*] Oh look! My feet! [*And indeed her little white feet are bare!*]

ASTOLAINE. [*After a pause.*] Oh, I don't think it matters. The Prince is a gentleman, and no gentleman would look at a lady's feet except to admire them.

SNOW WHITE. But I'd be different.

ASTOLAINE. Then let's *all* take off our shoes and stockings.

ROSALYS. Of course!
> [*Immediately they plump down on the floor. But they have hardly begun when a trumpet sounds from the terrace.*

SNOW WHITE. There's the Prince now!

ASTOLAINE. We can't stay here. Let's run into the anteroom to finish.

SNOW WHITE. I am so afraid something may happen. Really I ought not to, but I *do* so want to see him!

MAIDS OF HONOUR. Hurry! Hurry! dear Princess! [*And they hasten off into the anteroom, drawing* SNOW WHITE *with them.*]
> [*They are only just in time, for music sounds on the terrace, and the throne-room fills with* DUKES *and* DUCHESSES (*none of lower rank are allowed*) *all in*

*their best robes and Sunday coronets.
Then on struts* SIR DANDIPRAT, *more important and puffy than ever.*

SIR DANDIPRAT. [*Announcing.*] His Highness, Prince Florimond, Heir Apparent to the Kingdom of Calydon.

[*The* PRINCE *appears, followed by his
pages,* VALENTINE *and* VIVIAN. *He is
a handsome, manly youth, dressed in
blue and gold. He bows politely to the
kneeling* DUKES *and* DUCHESSES *as* SIR
DANDIPRAT *ushers him to the throne.*

SIR DANDIPRAT. I regret, your Highness, that
the Queen hasn't quite finished doing her hair; but
she will be here in a moment. Meantime, may the
Maids of Honour entertain your Highness with a
little dance?

THE PRINCE. It would give me great pleasure.

SIR DANDIPRAT. It is a very simple dance, your
Highness; but considering their youth, the . . .
[*But he stops because his eye falls upon a little pink*

shoe that GUINIVERE *has left behind.   He picks it up, hides it under his coat-tails and stumbles on.*] . . . the young persons do it very . . . er . . . very . . . [*And now he spies a stocking, and in hiding that the clumsy little man lets the shoe fall. This confuses him still more, but he goes on.*] er, very creditably indeed . . . [*And he sees a garter! This completes his embarrassment.   He forgets the rest of his speech altogether, and cries:*] Really they will drive me distracted! And where *are* they now? [*He dives about among the* DUKES *and* DUCHESSES *hunting for them, just as they appear in the doorway.*] Ah, here you are! Well, begin your dance at once! [*And off he puffs to find the* QUEEN, *wiping his forehead alternately with shoe and stocking as he goes.*]

> [*The* MAIDS OF HONOUR *begin their* GA-VOTTE.   *They are all veiled and all bare-footed, so that you couldn't tell* SNOW WHITE *from the others unless you happened to know that she was dressed in silver and white.   But there is something about her that attracts the young*

PRINCE *from the first; and as the dance*
progresses he becomes so interested that
he comes down from the throne to watch
her more closely. As the first figure
ends he is close beside her.

THE PRINCE. [*To* SNOW WHITE.]
In the measure to ensue,
Lady, may I dance with you?

SNOW WHITE. [*Giving him her hand.*]
Sir, could any maid withstand
Such a flattering command?

THE PRINCE.
Then I ask another grace,
Won't you please unveil your face?

SNOW WHITE. [*Hesitating, and then,*]
Yes, if secret it may be,
Secret between you and me.
[*The second figure of the Dance begins,*
SNOW WHITE *now dancing with the*
PRINCE. *Once in awhile we overhear*
what they are saying.

SNOW WHITE. [*Playfully.*]
  You look at me as if—we bow—
  You'd never seen my face till now.

THE PRINCE.
  Do you think I could forget
  If we two *had* ever met?

SNOW WHITE.
  Yet, in silence, side by side,
  Once we sat—until I cried!

THE PRINCE. [*Puzzled.*]
  Now I fear 'twill be my heart
  That will weep when we must part.

SNOW WHITE. [*Embarrassed.*]
  Now we turn and bow. Dear me!
  You don't know this dance, I see.

THE PRINCE.
  Can I think to bow and turn
  When I'm learning what I learn?
    [*The Dance ends, and a trumpet sounds to
    announce the coming of the* QUEEN.
      [42]

SCENE I

But the PRINCE *still holds* SNOW WHITE's *hand.*

SNOW WHITE.

There's the trumpet! I must fly!

Please, my hand, sir, and—good-bye!

THE PRINCE. [*Detaining her.*]

I don't even know your name!

Don't go yet—I'll take the blame!

SNOW WHITE.

Oh, I can't, nor tell you why!

Please! I beg you! Let me fly!

[*And she runs off, surrounded by the*
MAIDS OF HONOUR *who have been terribly frightened lest the* QUEEN *should
spy her.*

THE PRINCE. [*Gazing after her.*]

Do you think to steal my heart,

Little thief, and *so* depart?

Nay, I'll follow, fast and true,

Till I find my heart and you!

[SIR DANDIPRAT *appears on the terrace.*

[43]

SIR DANDIPRAT. [*Announcing.*] Her Majesty the Queen!

> [*To a crash of music and blare of trumpets* QUEEN BRANGOMAR *enters. She is dark, languorous and very beautiful. She wears her crown; and her long robes are embroidered in the blues and greens of the peacock's tail. She holds out a jewelled hand for* PRINCE FLORIMOND *to kiss, and then sweeps to the throne.*

THE QUEEN. So you are Prince Florimond? I'm sorry you chose to-day to come. I'm not looking my best.

THE PRINCE. [*Politely.*] I have always heard of Queen Brangomar as the most beautiful . . .

THE QUEEN. [*Interrupting rudely.*] Of course, of course! I am told you bring me a message from your father. What is it?

THE PRINCE. This letter. I don't know its contents, your Majesty.

THE QUEEN. [*Reading the letter.*] Your

father writes that if you *did* know it might embarrass you. M-m-m-m-m . . . wretched handwriting. "My son Florimond, now of an age to marry . . ."

THE PRINCE. [*Startled.*] Marry?

THE QUEEN. So your foolish old father is intending to marry you off, is he? I hope he isn't thinking of *me*. How many proposals would that make this week, Dandiprat?

SIR DANDIPRAT. Eleven, your Majesty—including those from the lunatic asylums.

THE QUEEN. [*Still reading.*] What's this? To "his cousin the Princess Snow White"! To Snow White! [*She rises in anger, crushing the letter.*] To Snow White! [*Then, trying not to betray her jealousy, and with a bitter laugh, she reseats herself.*] Really, my dear Florimond! of course I regret to say so, but Snow White isn't a *possible* choice. I'm sorry to disappoint you.

THE PRINCE. [*Interrupting.*] But you don't, I . . .

[45]

THE QUEEN. *I* was speaking! Snow White is most malicious and ill-tempered; and so stupid and common that she prefers to associate with kitchen-maids. Indeed, I believe she's in the kitchen at this very moment. She wouldn't do for you at all. Are not these the facts, Sir Dandiprat?

SIR DANDIPRAT. [*Hesitating.*] Well, your Majesty, . . . perhaps . . .

THE QUEEN. [*Sternly.*] Are not these the *facts*, Sir Dandiprat?

SIR DANDIPRAT. [*Crushed.*] They are, your Majesty.

THE PRINCE. Your Majesty has made me very happy!

THE QUEEN. Happy? I supposed . . .

THE PRINCE. Five minutes ago such an account of Snow White would have made me miserable, for even as a little boy I always dreamed of marrying my cousin when I grew up. But *now*—oh, will your Majesty help me if I confess?

THE QUEEN. Help you? How?

THE PRINCE. You see I've fallen in love with some one else meantime.

THE QUEEN. Meantime? When?

THE PRINCE. Here, just now, in this very room. She is the most beautiful . . .

THE QUEEN. [*With a pleased laugh.*] Oh, my poor boy! Really, I'm so much older than you . . .

THE PRINCE. [*With boyish frankness.*] Oh, not your Majesty. She's one of Snow White's Maids of Honour.

THE QUEEN. A Maid of Honour? You don't mean to say you want to *marry* one of them! Your father would never consent. They're nice girls, and come of quite respectable families—daughters of dukes and earls and that class—but you can only marry a Princess.

THE PRINCE. I'd marry her without my father's consent, even if we had to set up house-keeping in a poor cottage!

THE QUEEN. Don't be heroic! What is the young paragon's name?

THE PRINCE. She . . . she didn't tell me. We danced together, that was all.

THE QUEEN. [*Sarcastically.*] Are you quite sure you would even know her again?

THE PRINCE. Your Majesty is unkind!

THE QUEEN. Apparently the only way to discover the young person is to summon *all* the Maids of Honour. [*She motions* SIR DANDIPRAT, *who hurries off.*] I am curious to know your taste. Stand here by me and point her out when she comes.

> [SIR DANDIPRAT *reappears in the doorway and introduces the* MAIDS OF HONOUR, *one by one. As each* MAID *is named she curtsies to the* PRINCE.

SIR DANDIPRAT. The Maids of Honour. The Lady Rosalys. The Lady Amelotte. The Lady Ermengarde. The Lady Guinivere. The Lady Christabel. The Lady Astolaine. The Lady Ursula. The Lady Linnette.

[48]

THE PRINCE. [*After a pause of astonishment.*] But she's not there! There was another—!

THE QUEEN. Another? Eight—that is all.

SIR DANDIPRAT. [*Counting his fingers.*] Only eight, your Highness.

THE PRINCE. But there *was* another!

THE QUEEN. [*Suspiciously.*] Another? What was she like?

THE PRINCE. Her hair was black as polished ebony, her skin was whiter than new fallen snow, her lips were redder than a drop of blood!

THE QUEEN. [*In a terrible voice.*] Snow White! Summon Snow White!

    [SNOW WHITE *appears timidly in the entrance. I suspect she had been listening behind the curtains.*

SNOW WHITE. I am here, your Majesty.

THE PRINCE. That is she! And oh, she is Snow White! *You* are Snow White! [*He rushes to kneel at her feet.*]

THE QUEEN. [*Her anger quite overcoming her as she sees* SNOW WHITE's *changed appearance.*] Snow White! You! you dared! [*She rushes toward the little* PRINCESS, *but suddenly, half way, she falters and falls fainting.*]

SIR DANDIPRAT. [*Hopping about in great excitement.*] The Queen has fainted! The Queen has fainted! Oh, this is *most* important! Princess, Princess, see what you've done! Take her away, take her away! [*The* MAIDS OF HONOUR *lead* SNOW WHITE *away; and* SIR DANDIPRAT *turns to the astonished* PRINCE.] Most deplorable! Would your Highness withdraw to the terrace until the Queen recovers? It's most distracting. Air, air! Out of the room, everybody! Give her air!

> [*The* PRINCE *and the* COURTIERS *hurry
> out of the room. But no sooner is the*

SCENE I

QUEEN *alone with* SIR DANDIPRAT *than she recovers from her swoon.*

SIR DANDIPRAT. Shall I fan your Majesty? Oh, I hope . . .

THE QUEEN. Where is the Prince?

SIR DANDIPRAT. Waiting on the terrace, your Majesty.

THE QUEEN. Keep him there till I ring.

SIR DANDIPRAT. Oh, pray don't anger him! Gain time! Gain time!

THE QUEEN. Get out, you idiot! [*This rude exclamation so startles* SIR DANDIPRAT *that he stumbles backwards up the terrace steps, and waddles out of sight as fast as his fat legs will carry him.*]

THE QUEEN. [*Alone.*] The Witch! Witch Hex! I must summon her. She must help me now. [*She draws the curtains over both entrances so that she may not be seen at her magic.*] What

[51]

was the spell! Ah, I remember! [*In a hushed mysterious voice she chants.*]

THE SPELL

From my eyebrow pluck a hair,
 E—burrimee *boo*-row.
Blow it high up in the air,
 E—burrimee hock.
Where it lands a circle trace,
 E—burrimee *boo*-row.
Three times pace about the space,
   And
 Knock, knock, knock!
[*As she knocks smoke rises from the circle*
 she has traced, and there is a sound of
 distant thunder.
Thunder says the spell grows warm,
 E—burrimee *boo*-row.
Now I speak the mystic Charm,
 E—burrimee boo!

THE CHARM

Ee, Eye-*sof*-o-gos. Ee, Eye-sof-a-*giddle!*
Ee, Eye-*sof*-o-gos. Ee, Eye-sof-a-*giddle.*

Ee, Eye-*sof*-o-gos!

Ee, Eye-sof-o-*lof*-o-gos!

Ee, Eye-*sof*-o-gos!

Ee, Eye-sof-a-*giddle!*

[*The Charm sounds like nonsense; but it must be true magic, for the smoke increases as she chants it, and the thunder comes nearer.*

The spell's wound up, the charm is clear!

I summon thee, Witch Hex, appear!

[*Lo! through the smoking circle in the floor,* WITCH HEX *does appear. She looks exactly like all witches in fairy-tale pictures, with her black, pointed hat, red cloak, and crutched stick. It is evident that she is in a bad temper.*

THE WITCH.   Here, help me out, help me out!
[*The* QUEEN *assists her out of the smoking circle.*]
What's the meaning of this?   I'm getting tired of being called up by you night and day.   Last time I was in my night-gown, and it was snowing too.   I was an idiot to teach you that spell.   Whatever is the trouble now?

THE QUEEN. Don't be angry, dear godmother. You know how much I love you!

THE WITCH. Stuff! You don't love me. You dont' love anybody but yourself. That's the matter with you. If you only knew the trouble I have to take to keep you beautiful! Your disposition keeps wearing through. If I should once say, "Bang! no more charms for that wretched Brangomar," how would you look then? [*She chuckles at the thought.*] I believe you'd be uglier than I am.

THE QUEEN. I know, I know, dear Hex, but you wouldn't!

THE WITCH. Don't be too sure. Just summon me once too often, and you may find out how it feels to be the *ugliest* woman in the Seven Kingdoms.

THE QUEEN. Oh, tell me I am still the most beautiful!

THE WITCH. You look all right to me. But I warn you. I'm using my strongest magic now. You'd be much safer if you'd try to be good once in a while. Well, whom are you jealous of *this* time?

THE QUEEN. Snow White.

THE WITCH. Snow White? She's only a child!

THE QUEEN. So I thought till to-day, when I saw her for the first time prettily dressed.

THE WITCH. Well, why in the name of my cat Fiddle, did you dress her up?

THE QUEEN. I didn't. She tricked me.

THE WITCH. Who thought she was fairer than you?

THE QUEEN. Prince Florimond. He wants to marry her.

THE WITCH. Prince Florimond? Pooh! Mere boy! Probably said it to plague you, knowing your wretched disposition. But I've brought something with me this time that may help to keep you quiet. Just had time to snatch it when I felt you spelling away. It's a Magic Mirror.

[*She takes from her pocket and holds before* QUEEN BRANGOMAR'S *dazzled eyes
a hand mirror, carved from a single crystal. It glows and gleams like an opal.*

THE QUEEN. [*Seizing the Mirror and gazing
into it.*] Magic! . . . [*But suddenly she cries out
in horror.*] Oh!

THE WITCH. Ah, you see! Reflects you as you
really are. If I stopped my spells *that's* what
you'd look like. Now it makes me quite decent
looking. That's because my character's better.

THE QUEEN. Oh, the hateful thing! I never
saw anything so terrible. Why, I looked almost
funny! Take it away! Take it away!

THE WITCH. Wait! That's not all its magic.
Hold it in your hand and say:

Mirror, Mirror, in my hand,
Who's the fairest in the land?

and it will answer truthfully.

THE QUEEN. [*Snatching the Mirror, but shut-*

ting her eyes that she may not see her reflection.]
Oh, let me try!

> Mirror, Mirror, in my hand,
> Who's the fairest in the land?

THE WITCH.   Listen!
> [*There is a faint strain of music, and then
> a clear far-away voice that sounds like
> crystal bells, sings:*

SNOW WHITE

The Mirror's Song

SCENE I

You who hold me in your hand,
You were fairest in the land;
But, to-day, I tell you true,
Snow White is more fair than you!
[*With a scream of rage the* QUEEN *would
dash the Mirror to the floor, but the*
WITCH *rescues it just in time.*

THE WITCH. Stop! Stop! Stop! Gracious!
Listen to me, now. If you ever break that Mirror
you will become as ugly as you really are—and for
life, too! None of my spells can beauty you
again either, for the Mirror is made with those same
charms. [*Scornfully.*] I thought you knew
enough common, every-day magic for that!

THE QUEEN. [*Pacing up and down, weeping
with rage.*] But Snow White is more beautiful
than I! Snow White is more beautiful than I!

THE WITCH. [*Mocking her.*] Snow White is
more beau-hoo-hoo-tiful than I? Stop that waul-
ing.

THE QUEEN. But I can't bear it! Oh, make a spell and turn her ugly—as ugly as a toad!

THE WITCH. Won't! Refuse to make any more bad spells. If you can't bear the sight of her why not send her away somewhere,—say to boarding-school.

THE QUEEN. But she'd come back.

THE WITCH. Why should she? Suppose at boarding-school she gets mumps or freckles, or whatever those children's diseases are, and dies of it.

THE QUEEN. Oh, I see! You'll make a spell and give her the disease.

THE WITCH. No, no, no! Won't do any more bad magic, I tell you. You must contrive to have her lost on the *way* to boarding-school, and then just tell some tarradiddle to explain why she never comes back—and there you are! Everything permanently settled, and a little peace for me I hope.

THE QUEEN. I might! I could send Berthold,

"MIRROR, MIRROR IN MY HAND,
WHO'S THE FAIREST IN THE LAND?"

my Huntsman, as if he were taking her to school, and then . . . oh! . . . in the deep forest . . . [*She whispers,*] he shall put her to death!

THE WITCH. [*Starting.*] Goodness-gracious-mercy-me! I never suggested anything like that! Why I hear she's quite a nice child.

THE QUEEN. I shall never know a happy hour while she's alive!

THE WITCH. Well, there's no arguing with *you.* But can you trust your Huntsman?

THE QUEEN. I know a way to make him obey.

THE WITCH. Glad you know something! And look here, if you're *resolved* to have Snow White killed there's a little favour you might do me. I'm making a new spell that is really hard magic,—a hair restorer that will really restore hair. Want it for my own personal use. [*She pops off her cap and shows a perfectly bald head.*] I'd about given it up for want of the last ingredient—the heart of a nice young girl. Now I wouldn't harm a nice young girl myself for anything; but if you're de-

termined to dispose of Snow White I'd be obliged
for her heart.

THE QUEEN. I promise. Berthold shall bring
it to me as a proof. And now good-bye, dear Hexy.
I must summon him at once.

THE WITCH. Hm! It's always, "Good-bye,
dear Hexy," as soon as I've done what you want.
I'm afraid you don't love me for myself alone, dear
Brangomary! But I'm as glad to go as you are to
have me. Say the "Quick Spell" and get me off.
Ready!

> [*The* QUEEN *and the* WITCH *join hands,*
> *shut their eyes and chant in chorus.*

THE QUICK SPELL

THE QUEEN *and* WITCH.
> Bangaboo-bar;
> Bangaboo whack;
> Crow eat sun,
> Make all black!
> Mar-*oom*-bah!
> [*Everything suddenly becomes black. In*

*the darkness the two voices are still
heard, chanting:*

Bangaboo-bar;
Bangaboo-whack;
Mole dig hole,
Witch go back,
Mar-*oom*-bah!

[*There is a queer sound, something like a
very small earthquake. Then only the
QUEEN's voice is heard.*

THE QUEEN.

Bangaboo-bah;
Bangaboo whack;
Witch is gone,
Sun come back,
Mar-*oom*-bah!

[*The light returns as suddenly as it went.
The* WITCH *has vanished. Quite
calmly the* QUEEN *goes to the bell-cord.*

THE QUEEN. Let me see. I ring three times for
the Huntsman. [*She rings; but it is* SIR DANDI-
PRAT *who enters.*]

SIR DANDIPRAT. Your Majesty rang for me?

THE QUEEN. Not for you, idiot, for Berthold. Give me a minute alone with him and then summon the Prince and Snow White. Off with you!

> [SIR DANDIPRAT *hurries away, just as* CHIEF HUNTSMAN BERTHOLD *enters.* BERTHOLD *is tall and big. He has a thick, square beard and a kind, ruddy face.*

THE QUEEN. Berthold, I have a task for you.

BERTHOLD. I hope it is to take you a-hunting, your Majesty. Your forests are full of game, wild pigs, deer—indeed there may be even a unicorn or two.

THE QUEEN. It's other game I propose this time, Berthold. You have been a faithful Chief Huntsman. Suppose I promote you to be Lord High Admiral? As we have no navy the duties will be light.

BERTHOLD. Oh, your Majesty, how can I thank you?

THE QUEEN. It depends upon your carrying out a task with absolute obedience.

BERTHOLD. Give me a chance to show my gratitude.

THE QUEEN. Come nearer. The Princess Snow White is to set out for boarding-school this afternoon. You will conduct her. At the western gates, you will take the old road that turns to the left . . .

BERTHOLD. But, your Majesty, that road leads into the deep wood.

THE QUEEN. You will take *that* road. When you have come to the very heart of the forest—then [*and she hisses the words*] you will kill the Princess.

BERTHOLD. [*Springing back.*] Never, your Majesty, never!

THE QUEEN. It is my command. She has disobeyed me. She must be punished.

BERTHOLD. Kill Snow White? My late King's

daughter, the loveliest maid in the Seven Kingdoms? I would slay myself first! There is no
man in your dominions base enough to do such a
deed. Pray dismiss me! [*He turns to go.*]

THE QUEEN. [*In a terrible voice.*] Wait! I
have a surer means to command your obedience.
You have six small children I believe?

BERTHOLD. [*Wonderingly.*] Yes, your Majesty.

THE QUEEN. Suppose I lock your six children
in the great Grey Tower. Suppose I order that no
one shall take them food or drink.

BERTHOLD. Oh, your Majesty, have mercy!

THE QUEEN. Think! Can you not hear their
six small voices calling to you from the dark. "We
are hungry, Papa," they will cry; and they will beat
on the door with their little hands.

BERTHOLD. [*Sinking to the ground.*] Spare
me! Spare me!

THE QUEEN. At last they will be too weak to
[66]

cry or beat. Then, when all has grown still within the Tower, I will say, "Berthold, here is the key. Go and see how Queen Brangomar punishes disobedience."

BERTHOLD. [*Rising, with a cry.*] Oh, I will obey, your Majesty! Heaven forgive me, but I cannot let my children starve!

THE QUEEN. That's *much* better, Berthold. You understand clearly?

BERTHOLD. Alas! Too well!

THE QUEEN. Oh, what a tone of voice. Remember the motto: "A task cheerfully done is well done." And, oh, I almost forgot. You must bring me Snow White's heart, before midnight, as a proof. Here comes the Prince. *Do* try to look more pleasant.

> [PRINCE FLORIMOND *returns, ushered in by* SIR DANDIPRAT, *and followed by all the* COURTIERS.

THE PRINCE. I hope your Majesty has recovered.

THE QUEEN. Quite, thank you. I beg everybody's pardon. Something I had for lunch, no doubt. [*To* SIR DANDIPRAT.] Where is the Princess Snow White?

SNOW WHITE. [*Appearing.*] I am here, your Majesty.

THE QUEEN. My dear Snow White, Prince Florimond has come to ask your hand in marriage. What do you say?

SNOW WHITE. [*Drooping her head.*] What may I say?

THE QUEEN. Have you any reasons against it?

SNOW WHITE. [*Softly.*] None, your Majesty.

THE QUEEN. I was obliged to tell him how unfitted you are at present to become a Queen. Indeed, I've long been thinking of sending you away to some select boarding-school for backward Princesses. This seems the opportunity. You will remain at the school for a year and a day.

THE PRINCE. [*Exclaiming.*] Oh, your Majesty!

THE QUEEN. [*Firmly.*] And the Prince must promise not to see or write to you until the end of that time.

THE PRINCE. That seems too hard!

THE QUEEN. Otherwise, I shall refuse my consent. Do you agree?

THE PRINCE. Since I must.

THE QUEEN. Then *that's* settled! Return here one year and one day hence, and we can then [*and here she means more than she says,*] discuss the engagement. Now, Snow White, bid farewell to Prince Florimond. [*The* PRINCE *starts forward to kiss* SNOW WHITE'S *hand, but the* QUEEN *intervenes.*] No, no! A respectful bow, and a curtsey, will be quite sufficient. Good-bye, Florimond. Hasten back to your father.

[*So poor* PRINCE FLORIMOND *bows himself out, followed by his* PAGES; *but he looks*

back at SNOW WHITE *as long as he can
see her.*

THE QUEEN. [*Continuing.*] Now, Snow White,
I've arranged all the details about the boarding-
school. You must leave immediately or you won't
arrive before night-fall. Berthold will conduct
you. Say your good-byes quickly.

SNOW WHITE. Thank you so much, your Maj-

esty, I'm not quite sure that
I want to be a queen, but I
should like to be a well-
educated princess. I'm
very grateful. [*She tries
to take the* QUEEN's *hand,
but the* QUEEN *withdraws
it hastily.*]

THE QUEEN. You are
keeping Berthold waiting.
Off with you at once.

SNOW WHITE. [*Turning to her* MAIDS OF HON-
OUR.] Good-bye, my little playmates! Good-bye,

[70]

Amelotte and Ermengarde and Christabel and Rosalys. Don't cry, Rosalys, it will only be a year; and I promise not to come back so grown-up and princessy that you won't recognise your Snow White. Good-bye, dear ladies and gentlemen who have all been so good to me. I kiss you all!

> [*She blows them a kiss. Then, slipping her little hand into Berthold's big one, she says:*

Now Berthold!

> [*And* BERTHOLD *and the* PRINCESS SNOW WHITE *go off along the terrace toward the deep forest as*

THE CURTAIN FALLS

Scene II

In the Forest

Great trees meet over a wild and overgrown path.
It is after sunset, and the light is fading fast. A
small BROWN BIRD *flies above the path, chirping*
a little call, and perches in a tree just out of sight.
SNOW WHITE *running gaily, follows the* BIRD.

SNOW WHITE. Yes, little brown bird, I hear
you. You want another answer? Wait until I
get my breath. [*She whistles an imitation of the
bird's call.*] What? Flying on again, as soon as
you've made sure I've heard? Where are you trying to lead us? [*She calls back to* BERTHOLD.]
Berthold, there's the brown bird again. He seems
to be trying to get me to follow him. He's perched
on that tree now waiting for me to come up. [*The*

Bird *calls again, and* Snow White *tries to imitate the call in words.*] "Come, Snow White, come, Snow White!" Is that what you are trying to say? I'm coming! I'm coming! [*And she runs on, following the* Bird.]

> [Berthold *comes into sight. As he sees how lonely the spot is, and how dark with the shadows of the great trees, he halts irresolutely and murmurs to himself.*]

Berthold. It may as well be here as anywhere. Mile after mile you have put it off till the next turn or some more shadowed spot. But that is no kindness to the Princess. Remember your own children, man! It must be here! [*He calls after* Snow White—*and his voice is hoarse.*] Princess! Come back!

Snow White. [*Answering.*] What is it, Berthold? You want me? [*She runs back and slips her hand into his.*] There's the bird again. He seems to know the way better than you do. Do you think *he* can know that I'm going to boarding-

[76]

"THERE'S THE BIRD AGAIN. HE SEEMS TO KNOW THE WAY
BETTER THAN YOU DO"

school? [*The bird calls again, and she answers,*] Don't be so impatient! I shall stay with Berthold just as long as I like! He's a *much* older friend of mine than you are. What did you want, Berthold?

BERTHOLD. Oh, dear Princess . . . [*But he cannot go on.*]

SNOW WHITE. Why are you so pale? Have you hurt yourself? [*She tries to take his hand again, but he draws it away.*] Oh, you're angry with *me?* Something I did or said hurt your feelings? I didn't mean to. Please forgive me!

BERTHOLD. Forgive *you*, Princess! [*He kneels before her, and cries out in anguish.*] Say you can forgive me!

SNOW WHITE. [*Wonderingly.*] Forgive you? For what? [*She tries to raise his bowed head, that she may see his face.*] What is it, Berthold?

BERTHOLD. Don't look at me, Princess! Don't look at me! [*He folds his arms about her, and hides his face in her dress.*]

[77]

SNOW WHITE. Oh, whatever it is, tell me! I'm afraid!

BERTHOLD. The Queen . . .

SNOW WHITE. The Queen?

BERTHOLD. The Queen . . . has commanded me to . . . kill you . . . here . . . in this forest . . . now!

SNOW WHITE. [*Looking down at him in won-der.*] Kill me? I don't under-stand. You're taking me to school! . . . Oh, you're *joking!* I call that a silly joke, stupid old Berthold—a very silly joke. Look at me! No, *look* at me! [*Slowly he raises his head. She reads the truth in his face, and with a cry springs from him.*] Oh, it's true, it's true! I know it! That was why the Queen . . .! But you won't, will you? See, Berthold, I don't run away.

I come right to you. I creep into your arms. You won't hurt me, will you?

BERTHOLD. Oh, my darling! If it were my life alone that were at stake I would suffer any torture rather than harm a hair of your beloved head. But the Queen . . .

SNOW WHITE. Oh, you mean—that the Queen will kill you, unless . . .?

BERTHOLD. Not me, Princess, but my children. She has shut them up in the Grey Tower, and she will starve them to death . . .

SNOW WHITE. Oh, Berthold! [*Then after a little pause, she goes on softly.*] I know your little children. They have blue eyes and yellow hair. I've played with them. She would do it, too. [*She thinks a moment; then with sudden resolution, goes on.*] Kiss me good-bye, Berthold. I couldn't *live* and think of your children. See, I'm not crying—I'm not even very frightened. I'll turn away and shut my eyes. But please be quick!

BERTHOLD. [*Staggers to his feet and makes a fumbling movement for his knife; but as he touches it he sinks down again with a cry.*] I cannot, Princess, I cannot!

SNOW WHITE. But you must, Berthold! How else can you save your children?

BERTHOLD. [*Sobbing.*] I will find some way —some way.

SNOW WHITE. No, it's not possible, Berthold!

BERTHOLD. It's not possible for me to—kill— your Highness.
[*There is a silence.*]

SNOW WHITE. Berthold, considering the way the Queen has behaved do you think it would be very wrong to tell her a story?

BERTHOLD. [*Dazed.*] Wrong?

SNOW WHITE. Because if it weren't wrong, mightn't you *tell* her that you'd killed me without doing it?

BERTHOLD. But the proof! She has commanded me to bring her your—heart—before midnight.

SNOW WHITE. My heart? I've never seen a heart. I don't suppose a little piece of beef-steak would look at all like it, would it?

BERTHOLD. No, but . . . [*He springs up.*] Why not the heart of some beast! I might catch a wild pig here in the forest, and . . . [*Suddenly his voice drops.*] But no! I couldn't leave you here alone. You would starve.

SNOW WHITE. Couldn't I live like the birds, on berries?

BERTHOLD. But the winter will come—and—oh, your Highness, there are savage beasts in this wood.

SNOW WHITE. I haven't seen one;—not a living creature but my little brown bird.

BERTHOLD. It was daytime and I was with you; but it is growing dark, and at night . . .

SNOW WHITE. But if you don't take the heart to the Queen before midnight you know what she will do. The most savage beast would be less cruel. And you must catch the wild pig before it is too dark to see.

BERTHOLD. No! I dare not leave your Highness!

SNOW WHITE. [*Pretending to be struck with a new idea.*] Berthold, could you find this place again?

BERTHOLD. Find it? Every inch of the way is branded on my brain!

SNOW WHITE. Then to-morrow hide some food in your tunic and come back again, and we can plan. You might build me a little hut, and bring me food every day like a mother-bird, and I could live a little lone forest Princess.

BERTHOLD. [*Slowly.*] I might . . . but . . .

SNOW WHITE. Oh, please! There is *no* other hope, is there?

BERTHOLD. None that I can see.

SNOW WHITE. Then hurry. It's getting darker every moment. Kiss me good-bye quickly. [*She puts her face up to his.*] Until to-morrow, dear Berthold!

BERTHOLD. My Princess! Heaven keep you! Until to-morrow!

[*He hastens away.*

SNOW WHITE. [*Calling after him.*] Good-bye, dearest Berthold! [*Then, to herself.*] Poor Berthold, does he think the Queen will ever let him out of her sight again? No, she will shut him up in prison for fear that he might tell. He will never come back! Good-bye forever, Berthold! [*A sudden terror seizes her.*] Oh, it's good-bye forever, everybody! [*She starts after him, crying,*]

Berthold, come back, come back! [*But remember-ing, she clasps her hands over her mouth to stifle the cry.*] Hush! Snow White! Think of his children, think of his children! [*With a little moan, she sinks to the ground.*] But what shall I do? Where shall I go? I'm afraid—I'm afraid—afraid! [*And she hides her face among the leaves.*]

> [*The call of the little* BROWN BIRD *is heard almost overhead. At first* SNOW WHITE *does not hear, and the* BIRD *repeats the cry that sounds almost like "Come, Snow White!"*]

SNOW WHITE. [*Looking up in wonder.*] Oh little bird, are *you* still here? You haven't left me. I think you are my friend—the only friend I have in all this world now. [*The* BIRD *flies off a little way and then perches and repeats his call.*] Are you telling me to follow you, as you did before? But where shall I follow? I have nowhere to go. I wish I might live in your nest, little bird. [*Again the* BIRD *calls and* SNOW WHITE *rises and follows where he flies.*]   Yes, I will follow, I trust you.   [*She runs out of sight among the trees, calling softly as she goes.*]   I hear!   I am coming!   I am following, little brown bird!

THE CURTAIN FALLS

Scene III

In the House of the Seven Dwarfs

The Dwarfs' House is very tiny. It is built of rough stones and logs, and niched into a hillside in the depths of the great wood. It has but one room, two windows and a half door. Along one side of the room are ranged seven little beds of different sizes; on the other is a stone fireplace for cooking, and a rustic pump with a barrel under its spout to catch the water. In the middle of the stone floor stands a low table with seven places laid for supper. A single candle on the table lights the room. Through the window we see the forest, dim in the moonlight.

Presently the little BROWN BIRD *flies past, and perches on a branch just outside, still calling* SNOW WHITE *to follow him. They have come a*

*long way and she is very tired and hungry. But,
as she sees the little house, and realises at last
where the* BROWN BIRD *was leading her, she runs
up and peeps in through the window.*

SNOW WHITE. Oh, was it toward this light you
were leading me, brown bird? Why, it's a little
house! Are you flying away now? Please let me
thank you first:—see, I blow you a kiss! He's
gone. Perhaps birds don't like kisses; their faces
are so sharp. [*Calling after him.*] Good-bye, little friend! [*She looks cautiously through the
window into the house.*] What a queer little
room! Seven beds and all so small. There must
be lots of children in the family. Nobody with so
many children could be wicked. [*She calls.*]
May I come in? [*As there is no answer she knocks
at the door and then opens it a crack.*] Please,
good people, may I come in to rest—just for a moment? I'm lost in the forest. [*Still no answer.
She creeps into the room and looks about.*] Nobody at home. But they couldn't mind if I sat
down, just a minute. Oh, there is the children's

[90]

"I WISH I MIGHT LIVE IN YOUR NEST, LITTLE BIRD"

supper, all laid out. I'm so hungry! If I took just a bit—only a tiny bit—from each place, I'm sure they couldn't be angry. [*She goes to the table, and as she nibbles a morsel at each place she sings to herself.*]

SNOW WHITE

Eating Song

SCENE III

fork to break a mor-sel from this bar-ley cake, I'll steal one cher-ry

from these four, And not a sing-le mouth-ful more.

(She hesitates, then

with sudden decision:-) Quick

And not a sin-gle mouth-ful more

[93]

EATING SONG

A sip of water from this cup,
Of porridge just one tiny sup.
I'll take this little knife to spread,
A corner of the next one's bread;
And borrow this wee fork to break
A morsel from this barley cake.
I'll take one cherry from these four,—
But not a single mouthful more,
No, not a single mouthful more!

SNOW WHITE. Nobody *could* begrudge me that. But I'd like to do something to pay for my supper. [*She looks about.*] There's plenty to be done. It isn't at all a tidy house. [*She yawns, and then shaking herself.*] Wake up, Snow White! You mustn't get sleepy yet; not till the people come home. [*But she cannot quite stifle another yawn.*] There's a broom. Suppose I sweep a little. [*She begins to sweep, but the broom raises such a cloud of dust, that, coughing, she has to stop at once.*] Dear me, that only makes things worse. This floor needs a good scrubbing. I might make up the beds. [*She goes to the biggest bed; but she is so tired that she sits down on it a moment before beginning.*] This one looks as if it hadn't been made for years and years and years. I wonder if it's as humpy to lie on as it is to sit on. [*She lies down to try it.*] Oh, it's more . . . It's humpy and bumpy . . . and bumpy and humpy . . . and . . . [*Her voice trails away into silence. She has fallen asleep.*]

SNOW WHITE

Snow-white sleeps and the Dwarfs come in

Music by
Edmond Rickett, Op. 25

SCENE III

[*For a time all is quiet in the little room. Then, from far underground is a sound of distant knocking. It comes nearer till it sounds just under the house. Finally a great stone slab in the floor is pushed up slowly, and from an underground passage that leads from the house into the deep mines, six of the* SEVEN DWARFS *clamber up into sight.*

Their names are BLICK, FLICK, GLICK, SNICK, PLICK *and* WHICK. *They are very small—the tallest hardly above your waist—but they are extremely old, and their beards are long and grey. Each carries a lighted lantern and a pickaxe, and bears a heavy sack over his shoulder. As soon as the last one has climbed into the room they form in line, with* BLICK, *the eldest, at the head.*

BLICK. Now, brothers, evening roll-call! [*He calls his own name.*] Blick [*And answers.*] Here! [*Then he calls each of the others by*

name—] "Flick!" "Glick!" "Snick!" "Plick!" "Whick!" [*Last of all* BLICK *calls.*] Quee!
[*There is no answer. He re-*
peats.] Quee! [*Still no an-*
swer. BLICK *shakes his head*
sadly.] Late as usual! He's
been stealing again. Whatever shall we do with that
boy? [*All the* DWARFS *sigh*
and hang their heads with
shame at QUEE'S *conduct.*
But BLICK *goes on.*] Well,

brothers, what result of to-day's work? Half a
ton of gold nuggets for mine. [*He takes a hand-*
ful of enormous nuggets from his sack. The others
also exhibit their treasures as they name them.]

FLICK.   A hundred weight of silver dust.

GLICK.   Fifty pounds of diamonds.

SNICK.   A bushel of rubies.

PLICK.   A gallon of emeralds.

WHICK. A peck of opals.

BLICK. Fair, fair! But we ought to work longer hours.

FLICK. Yes, what's the good of coming home— except to sleep.

GLICK. And have supper.

FLICK. [*With scorn.*] Oh, that supper!

BLICK. I know, I know! It's wretched. If we cook it at night it's too hot to eat; if we cook it in the morning it's cold and dusty by night; but what else can we do?

GLICK. And I'd rather sleep underground than in those beds.

ALL. So would we!

BLICK. I know! They haven't been made for twelve years. But it doesn't pay to take time from digging diamonds to make beds, so what can we do?

ALL. [*Sighing.*] Nothing.

[100]

From an underground passage . . . six of the Seven
Dwarfs clamber up into sight

SNICK. But if we didn't come home to supper we wouldn't have to wash.

BLICK. [*Shocked.*] Oh, brothers! Washing is a duty. Hush! I think I hear Quee. [*They all cock their heads sidewise like robins and listen.*] Yes, that's Quee. He *has* been stealing again! We must scold him soundly.

FLICK. It never does any good.

BLICK. But we must bring him up in the way he should go. He is the youngest of us; he's only ninety-nine next April. Clear away and ready for him.

> [*They pile their sacks in a corner, and squat on the floor in a semi-circle, with* BLICK, *like a presiding judge, in the centre.*
> [QUEE *creeps up stealthily through the underground passage. He is much the smallest, but grey bearded like the rest. As he faces his brothers, one finger creeps*

[101]

into his mouth. BLICK *greets him sternly.*

BLICK. Quee, you are late again! [QUEE *nods.*] Been stealing as usual, I suppose? [QUEE *nods.*]

ALL. [*Shaking their fingers at him, reprovingly.*] Oh!

BLICK. You know it's wrong!

ALL. Very, very wrong! [QUEE *nods.*]

BLICK. Did anybody catch you at it? [QUEE *shakes his head.*] That's good—as far as it goes.

FLICK. Did you get me a mouse-trap? [QUEE *nods.*]

GLICK. And my candles? [QUEE *nods.*]

FLICK. And a pin? [QUEE *nods.*] I'm glad of that. I've never seen a pin.

BLICK. Of course you understand, Quee, that stealing is a sin, and that your conduct makes us very sad?

[102]

ALL. Very, very sad!

BLICK. Will you promise to reform, and never, never steal again . . .?

FLICK. [*Interrupting hastily.*] Wait, wait! Give him the list of things to get to-morrow first!

BLICK. Dear me, I almost forgot! Quee, tie a string around your finger to remember by. Now, what do you all want?

THE DWARFS. [*Speaking in rapid succession; each names one article.*]

A chain. A plane. A weather-vane.
A hat. A mat. A pussy-cat.
   A pound of brass.
   A pane of glass.
A crock. A lock. An eight-day clock.

A can. A pan. A palm-leaf fan.
A tack. A sack. An almanac.

[103]

A can of soup.

A chicken-coop.

A map. A cap. A snappy trap.

A pole. A bowl. A baker's roll.

A rake. A cake. A pound of steak.

A peck of meal.

A pickled eel.

A slate. A plate. A ten-pound weight.

BLICK. That's all for to-morrow. But remember, young man, if "it's a sin to steal a pin" how much worse it must be to steal a ten-pound weight. You appreciate that? [QUEE *nods sadly.*] Brothers, we shall have to correct him again to-morrow night. He is incorrigible.

ALL. [*Mournfully.*] In-cor-rig-ible!

BLICK. Now for the evening washing. Get the basin, Quee.

> [*Glad that his daily scolding is over,* QUEE *runs cheerfully and fetches a basin of water, a big sponge and a towel.*

BLICK. No flinching now, brothers. Line up!

Right faces! [*They all, except* QUEE, *stand close together, and thrust their faces over one another's shoulders, with eyes closed. Running down the line,* QUEE *washes all their right cheeks with one long sweep of his sponge.*] Reverse! [*cries* BLICK. *They all turn and face in the opposite direction; and* QUEE, *running up the line, washes all their other cheeks.*] Right faces! [*cries* BLICK. *With a single sweep of his towel,* QUEE *now dries all their right cheeks; and when* BLICK *commands* "Reverse," *he dries the opposite sides in the same neat and speedy way. And the evening washing is finished.*]

BLICK. There! That's over for another twenty-four hours.

ALL. Thank goodness!

BLICK. Oh come! It's quick and comparatively painless. Only—Quee gets dirtier and dirtier every year.

FLICK. But somebody must do it.

GLICK. He's the youngest.

WHICK. It's his duty.

BLICK. Nevertheless he's a disgrace to the family. [QUEE *bows his head in shame.*] I'm glad that you realise it, at least.

GLICK. And now [*with a heavy sigh*] supper!

ALL. [*Sadly.*] Supper!

FLICK. No hurry! It's been getting cold ever since breakfast.

> [*With lagging steps they march to the table, and are about to eat, when* BLICK *starts back in surprise.*

BLICK.
  I say!
  Some one's been drinking from my cup!

SNICK.
  Some one has eat my porridge up!

FLICK.
  And used my brand-new knife to spread
  A monstrous corner of Quee's bread!

[106]

SCENE III

PLICK.

Some one has used my fork.

GLICK.

　　　　　　　　　　　To break
A quarter off my barley-cake!

WHICK.

One cherry's missing from my four!

ALL.

And, goodness gracious, how much more?
　　　[They gaze at each other in amazement.

BLICK. [*Whispering.*] Brothers, there must be Robbers in the house!

FLICK.　Or Pirates.

GLICK.　Or Burglars.

BLICK.　Probably Burglars.　If so, they are under the beds; burglars always are.　Hush!　Let every man look under his own bed.
　　　[Each DWARF *creeps to his bed, and peers
　　　cautiously under it.　Then, one after*

*the other, they rise, shaking their heads
and saying,* "Nobody under my bed!"
"Nobody under my bed!" "Nobody
under my bed!" BLICK *is the last to
rise, but as he does so he sees* SNOW
WHITE *and cries, in a tense whisper*]
"But—there's something *in* it! Look,
brothers!"

[*In wonder, the* DWARFS *creep about*
BLICK'S *bed, and holding their lanterns
high, gaze down upon the sleeping*
SNOW WHITE. *An* "ah!" *of admiration
breaks from their lips.*

GLICK. [*Whispering.*] What is it?

FLICK. I know! It's a child.

BLICK. No, it's a girl. I saw one once.

FLICK. Well, girl *or* child, it's the most beautiful thing I ever saw.

GLICK. Or I. Is it tame, or will it fly away like a bird, when it wakes up?

[108]

SCENE III

FLICK. I've heard that children are quite tame; —and they can talk!

ALL. [*In rapture.*] Oh!

BLICK. But I tell you this isn't a child, it's a girl. I don't think *girls* can talk. [*They all heave a sigh of disappointment.*]

FLICK. I wish she'd stay with us just so that we could look at her.

BLICK. She won't.

GLICK. Why not?

BLICK. Of *course* she won't. Are we handsome, or young, or tall? In fact, aren't we dwarfs? [*They all hang their heads.*]

FLICK. But if we didn't tell her that?

BLICK. Flick, I wonder at you! Besides, she might find it out.

GLICK. She's beautifully white and clean. Look, she's had the broom; she's been trying to sweep.

FLICK. I can't bear to think of her leaving us.

GLICK. None of us can.

FLICK. I'm going to stay up all night just to watch her.

GLICK. Do you think there's any way we could persuade her to stay?

BLICK. I'm afraid not.

FLICK. Even if we laid presents on her bed?

BLICK. What kind of presents? Gold and diamonds?

FLICK. Oh, not *common* things like that; really valuable things like—my jack-knife!

BLICK. Oh, things like *that!* It might! But I'm afraid not.

FLICK. We might try anyhow. Let each man give the most valuable thing he has in the world.

> [BLICK *collects the gifts. Each* DWARF *names his present lovingly as he takes it from his pocket.*

[110]

SCENE III

BLICK. My thimble!

SNICK. My almanac.

PLICK. My empty bottle.

GLICK. And my pet frog.

BLICK. [*Laying the gifts gently on the foot of* SNOW WHITE'S *bed.*] There! that *may* help. But no! It's no use, brothers. There is Quee!

ALL. [*Hopelessly.*] Yes! There is Quee!

FLICK. We might hide him?

BLICK. She'd be sure to find him sooner or later.

GLICK. He might reform.

BLICK. But we never could pretend he wasn't dirty. He hasn't been washed for fifty years.

FLICK. [*With a sudden inspiration.*] Brothers, why not wash him now?

GLICK. We might!

ALL. We WILL!!

[111]

BLICK. Flick, you're a genius. But it must be done at once or he won't be dry by morning. Get the utensils.

BLICK. [*Marching to the pump.*]
    Here's the pump to douse him with!

SNICK. [*Fetching the basin.*]
    Here are suds to souse him with!

FLICK. [*Bringing the sponge.*]
    Here's the sponge to sop him with!

PLICK. [*Hurrying with the broom.*]
    Here's the broom to mop him with!

GLICK. [*Running with the soap.*]
    Here's the soap to scrub him with!

WHICK. [*Waving the towel.*]
    Here's the cloth to rub him with!
      [*They surround* QUEE, *who stands abashed, his finger in his mouth.*

BLICK. Quee, you are going to be . . .

SCENE III

ALL. [*In a tremendous whisper.*] WASHED!
[*They carry him to the barrel, plump him in with a great splash, and pump on him. Then, as they scrub and rub and soap and stir him about in the water, they chant in chorus:*

THE DWARFS.
Here's the pump to *douse* him with!
Here are suds to *souse* him with!
Here's the sponge to *sop* him with!
Here's the broom to *mop* him with!
Here's the soap to *scrub* him with!
Here's the cloth to *rub* him with!
Rub! Scrub! Mop! Sop! Souse! Douse!
Rub!
Scrub!
Mop!
Sop!
Souse!
Douse!
[*In their excitement they forget to be as quiet as they had meant to be, and* SNOW

WHITE *stirs in her sleep. Then she wakes, and sits up.*

SNOW WHITE. Where is this—? Oh, there are the children that live here. Why, they're *not* children. They have long beards! They're queer, little old men. *They'll* never let me stay with them. But I must tell them I'm here. [*She rises, and standing by the bed says shyly.*] I beg your pardon.

[*The* DWARFS *turn suddenly.*

SNOW WHITE. [*With a little curtsey.*] I'm sorry if I've disturbed you; but I was lost in the forest, and when I saw your house I was so tired and hungry that I came in and took a little food— without asking. Then I'm afraid I fell asleep. [*She waits for an answer, but the* DWARFS *gaze at her in silence, so she falters on.*] I'd pay for it, but I haven't any money. [*Again a silence.*] So all I can do is to say, "Thank you"—and "Good night." [*She moves reluctantly to the door. The* DWARFS *sigh deeply. She turns for a farewell curtsey.*] Thank you *very* much. [*She half shuts*

[114]

the door behind her, then re-opens it to repeat.]
Good night! [*There is no answer, except another heavy sigh from the* Dwarfs. *With sudden pity she bursts out.*] Oh, you're not *dumb*, are you?

Blick. [*Clearing his throat.*] No, we're not dumb; but you're a girl, aren't you?

Snow White. [*Wonderingly.*] Yes—I'm a girl.

Blick. And young?

Snow White. I'm not very old.

Blick. We don't know how to talk to young people.

Snow White. Well, most grown people begin, "Why, how you've grown!" And usually the next thing is, "How do you like your school?"

Blick. [*To* Snow White.] "How you've grown."

Flick. "How do you like your school?"

Snow White. [*Smiling, but a little embar-*
[115]

rassed.] Well—perhaps it *is* a little late for conversation. It's long past bedtime, isn't is?

BLICK. **Long** past.

SNOW WHITE. There are six of you and—seven beds, aren't there?

BLICK. [*Hastily putting the cover on the barrel.*] Yes, there are seven beds.

SNOW WHITE. Oh, before I go perhaps I ought to tidy the one I slept in. I didn't tumble it much. [*She goes to the bed.*] What are these things on it? [*She starts back.*] Oh! one's a frog. It's alive!

GLICK. He *was* my frog. He's perfectly tame.

SNOW WHITE. What a funny thing to put on a bed.

BLICK. [*Edging toward her eagerly.*] They were meant to be presents.

SNOW WHITE. Presents? Is it Christmas here?

BLICK. We don't know. We don't know what Christmas is.

SNOW WHITE. Oh—somebody's birthday?

FLICK. No, it's nobody's birthday.

SNOW WHITE. Then I don't see—?

BLICK. They were meant to be presents for *you*.

SNOW WHITE. For me?

FLICK. We were afraid you wouldn't like them.

BLICK. I knew you wouldn't like them.

SNOW WHITE. But I *do* like them. Do you mean that you're not angry with me,—that you don't dislike me so *very* much?

FLICK. *Dislike* you!

BLICK. We think you're the most wonderful thing we've ever seen!

SNOW WHITE. Oh, you darlings!—oh, I beg your pardon. Perhaps that wasn't respectful.

[117]

BLICK. Nobody ever called us "darlings" before, so we don't know.

FLICK. But it sounds nice.

SNOW WHITE. And you wouldn't mind if I should stay to-night,—only just to-night?

BLICK. We wouldn't mind if you should stay forever—only just forever!

SNOW WHITE. Forever?

FLICK. Oh, will you?

SNOW WHITE. Oh, will you *let* me? Please let me live with you! I could be so useful.

BLICK. But our housekeeping . . .

SNOW WHITE. That's just how I could be useful. I can cook and sew and sweep and brew and make beds, and—oh, lot's of things.

BLICK. [*Solemnly.*] Will you excuse us a moment, please? [*He calls the* DWARFS *together and whispers to them.*] Did I hear right? Did she say she would *stay?*

[118]

SCENE III

ALL. [*Eagerly.*] She did!

BLICK. [*Confused.*] Er—whatever shall we say?

ALL. [*Perplexed.*] *We* don't know.

BLICK. [*Turning again to* SNOW WHITE.] Er —could you tell us what it's usual to say when you're so glad that it almost *bursts* you?

SNOW WHITE. Would "Hip-hip-hurrah!" do?

BLICK. It *sounds* right. [*Slowly.*] Hip-hip-hurrah?

ALL. [*Solemnly trying the new word.*] Hip-hip-hurrah? [*Then deciding that it does fit their feelings, they shout in a joyous outburst.*] Hip-hip-hurrah!

SNOW WHITE. [*Clapping her hands.*] Oh, please, may I say, "Hip-hip-hurrah!" too? I am so glad and grateful.

ALL. Hip-hip-hurrah!!

SNOW WHITE. [*Remembering.*] But, oh—

you may not want me when I tell you who I am.
It may be dangerous . . .

BLICK. [*Hopefully.*] Do *you* steal?

SNOW WHITE. [*Smiling.*] No, not so bad as
that. My name is Snow White.

BLICK. It sounds extremely clean.

SNOW WHITE. This morning I was a Princess.
[*She sits on* BLICK'S *bed to tell her story. She is
growing drowsy again.*]

FLICK. What's a Princess?

SNOW WHITE. Why, the daughter of a king
and queen. My step-mother is Queen Brangomar.
[*More sleepily.*] She hates me so much that I'm
afraid there must be something horrid about me
. . . [*she is very drowsy now*] but I'm sure Prince
Florimond didn't not like me . . . for . . . [*She
sinks back onto the bed and her eyes close. The*
DWARFS *put their fingers to their lips. Then she
revives a little and murmurs,*] for a year and a
day . . . oh, what was I saying? I'm *so* sleepy.

SHE SITS ON BLICK'S BED TO TELL HER STORY

Please, mayn't I tell you to-morrow morning? All I can think of now is "good night!"

BLICK. [*Softly.*] Good night, Snow White!

SNOW WHITE. [*Almost asleep.*] Good night.

FLICK. Good night, Snow White.

SNOW WHITE. Good—night.

GLICK. Good night, Snow White.

SNOW WHITE. Good . . .

[*There is a silence.*

BLICK. [*Whispering.*] Brothers, she's asleep. But she'll stay, she'll stay!

ALL. [*Whispering.*] Hip-hip-hurrah!

FLICK. I'm so happy I'm sad!

GLICK. [*Wiping away a tear with his long beard.*] I'm so happy it's making me cry!

SNICK. We're all so happy! [*They all wipe their eyes with their beards.*]

BLICK. We mustn't wake her. Not a sound now. We'll be quietest in bed. [*Each* DWARF *creeps toward his bed.*]

BLICK. [*Puzzled.*] But she's in my bed! Well, I'll take Flick's.

> [*He moves to the next bed, jumps in, and pulls the clothes over his head,* (DWARFS *always sleep with the bedclothes over their heads*). *Of course each of the others has to move up one bed. As they pop in, one after another, and cover their heads they cry:*

FLICK. I'll take Glick's!

GLICK. I'll take Snick's!

SNICK. I'll take Plick's!

PLICK. I'll take Whick's!

WHICK. I'll take Quee's!

BLICK. [*Sitting up suddenly.*] Brothers, we've forgotten Quee! [*They all sit bolt upright. Then in a whisper they call.*]

SCENE III

ALL. Q-U-E-E! [*The cover over the water-barrel is pushed up, and* QUEE'S *head appears. He is very wet, but washed as clean and pink as a new doll.*]

BLICK. Quee, she'll stay, but you'll have to sleep in the barrel.

QUEE. Hip-hip-hurrah! [*He disappears again into the barrel, and*

THE CURTAIN FALLS

WHERE THE WITCH LIVES

WITCH HEX *lives in a queer dark place, somewhat like a cavern, with walls of soft black moss. Yet it can't be underground, for looking out through the single entrance that serves for both door and window you can see the moon, very big and low, and always shining day or night.*

A great fire blazes in the middle of the floor, and over it stands a boiling cauldron. Against the wall is a large chest, carved with strange signs, in which the WITCH *keeps her Magic Things.*

Curled up asleep by the fire lies her pet cat, FIDDLE. FIDDLE *is enormous for a cat—almost as big as a small boy. Presently he wakes, yawns and has a long stretch, shaking the last sleepiness out of both hind legs. Then he washes his face care-*

[127]

*fully, round and round, with his paw. He feels
hungry, so he rubs his stomach; but as that doesn't
do much good he looks about for something to eat.
A large tin with holes bored in the cover stands
on the chest, and he remembers seeing his mis-
tress sprinkle something from this over her food.
So he lies down on his back luxuriously, and, lick-
ing his chops, takes the tin in both hind paws and
shakes it vigorously over his open mouth. But
suddenly, with an enormous yowl, he leaps into
the air, coughing, blinking, sneezing and mewing
all at once. What he found was the* WITCH'S
pepper-pot!

*The pepper makes him feel extremely lively; and
now he spies a loose end of yarn dangling from
an old spinning-wheel that stands in a dark corner. He bounds to it and pats the swinging end
to and fro. But the wool catches on one of his
sharp claws and he cannot throw it off. He rolls
on the ground to break it, but the yarn is strong
and only binds him round and round. Now he is
frightened, and begins to run and whirl and
spring into the air; but with every movement the*

thread, unwinding from the wheel, wraps him closer and closer; and the more he spins and turns and somersaults head over heels, the more tangled he gets, till at last he cannot move a paw or even swing his indignant tail; and lies on his back a helpless, mewing bundle.

Fortunately at this moment there is a shadow across the moon, and WITCH HEX *flies home, riding on her broomstick, a basket on her arm.*

THE WITCH. [*Alighting and setting her broomstick away.*] There! Glad to be home at last. Where is Queen Brangomar? I thought she'd be here before me with Snow White's heart. I had to go half way to the Moon for the other ingredients for that magic hair-restorer; but I've got them all, safe in my basket. Where is that lazy-bones Cat of mine? [*She calls.*] Fiddle, Fiddle, Fiddle!

> [*The only answer is a faint mew from something like a huge ball of yarn in*

the corner. The WITCH *examines it, and then breaks into a laugh.*

THE WITCH. Well, Fiddle, whatever have you been up to now? Oh, ho! playing with my spinning-wheel? Well, you are a snarl. Wait—I'll unwind you!

> [*She seizes one end of the yarn and winds it into a ball, but so quickly that poor* FIDDLE, *at the other end, spins and whirls and revolves like a top as she unwinds him, and the* WITCH *laughs at his antics till the tears stream down her withered old cheeks. When he is free,* FIDDLE *has to sit in a corner and hold his head in both paws for dizziness; but, picking up her basket, the* WITCH *says:*

THE WITCH. Now come here and help me mix that magic hair restorer. We must stew all the other ingredients together before Brangomar comes.

> [*The* WITCH *and* FIDDLE *dance round and round the cauldron in a mystic circle;*

[130]

"We must stew all the other ingredients together before Brangomar comes"

SCENE IV

and as HEX *throws the various things she has collected into the boiling brew she sings:*

SNOW WHITE

The Magic Mixture

blast ___ that the Lit-tle Boy Blue ___ A tear of the

kit-tens, Who lost all their mit-tens, When they ___ be - gan to

cry; ___ A sniff from Miss Mar-y When she was con-

tra-ry; The plum from Jack Hor-ner's pie; ___ The

SNOW WHITE

plum ___ from Jack Hor-ner's Pie. ___

slice ___ of green cheese ___ from the Man in the Moon; The

SCENE IV

Tails ___ of the Three Blind Mice; A bone from the cup-board

Of old Moth-er Hub-bard; And lit-tle girls sug-ar and

spice; ___ A tick from the clock of Hickor-y, Dick-o-ry-

Dock; The tails ___ of the sheep of Bo - peep; ___ The

SCENE IV

THE MAGIC MIXTURE

A hair from the tail of the ride-a-cock Horse;
  A lace from the Old Woman's shoe,
     A bit of the tuffet
     Of Little Miss Muffet;
  The blast that the Little Boy Blue.
A tear of the Kittens who lost all their mittens
  When they began to cry.
     A sniff from Miss Mary
     When she was contrary;
  The Plum from Jack Horner's pie.

A slice of Green Cheese from the Man in the Moon;
  The tails of the Three Blind Mice;
     A bone from the cupboard
     Of Old Mother Hubbard;
  And little girls' sugar and spice.
A tick from the clock of hi-diccory Dock;
  The tails of the sheep of Bo-peep;
     The eye of the fly
     That saw Cock Robin die;
And a "baa" from the Baa-black Sheep.
       [When she has finished the mixture, the

WITCH *sniffs the steam from the cauldron, and then sips a little of the brew
from the ladle.*

THE WITCH. Tastes good,
and hot enough. Yes, the
ladle is red hot. Now that's
all except the heart. Fiddle,
set the kettle to cool.

[FIDDLE *takes the cauldron from over the
fire and sets it in the corner.*

THE WITCH. I'm chilly! [*She tucks up her
skirts and sits down comfortably on the blazing
fire.*] Ah, that feels good! Nothing to do now
but wait for Snow White's heart. But *then* you
shall see what you shall see—a beautiful head of
long, wavy hair. Ah, here's Brangomar at last.

[QUEEN BRANGOMAR *enters.* FIDDLE
bows low to her.

THE QUEEN. Sorry to be late, dear Hexy, but
Berthold never returned till morning, and then I
had to see personally to having him locked up in

[138]

the Grey Tower. He made a frightful fuss; but I
was afraid to trust him.

THE WITCH. Did he bring the heart?

THE QUEEN. Yes, here it is. Oh, how I hated
that child!

THE WITCH. Hair restorer's just ready for it.
Help me up. Don't like to sit on the fire *too* long.
I dosed off the other day and boiled over. Now the
heart. [*She takes it and hobbles to the cauldron.*]
Receipt says that when I add this the brew will
turn a beautiful pink. Then I dip in my head, and
presto! long and lovely hair. Now watch!

[*She drops the heart into the cauldron,
which steams vigorously.*

THE WITCH. [*Dancing with delight.*] See it steam!

THE QUEEN. But it's turning
green, not pink.

THE WITCH. So it is. Still, there can't be any
mistake; I was most careful. Well, here goes for

a handsome head of hair. You'll hardly know me when you see me again. [*She dips her head three times into the steaming cauldron, and then raises it proudly.*] How's that? Pretty fine, eh?

> [*Surely something has sprouted on the* WITCH's *bald pate. The* QUEEN *looks carefully, and then bursts into a peal of laughter; and* FIDDLE, *holding his sides, rolls on the ground in mirth.*]

THE WITCH. What are you laughing at? Feels very thick and curly. Stop that cackling!

THE QUEEN. [*Hardly able to speak.*] Oh, my dear Hex! Ha, ha, ha! You have—ha, ha, ha! —a headful of pig-tails!

THE WITCH. Pig-tails? Nonsense! It's short and curly.

THE QUEEN. Not pig-tails, Hexy. Your head is covered with little white, curly tails of pigs!

THE WITCH. Tails of pigs? Tails of pigs? [*She feels the growth carefully.*] By Hop-scotch,

[140]

they *are* pigs' tails! Stop laughing! If the joke's on anybody, it's on *you.* Instead of a *human* heart, your precious huntsman has brought back the heart of a pig; and Miss Snow White is alive at this moment. Ha, ha, for *you!*

THE QUEEN. [*Her laughter broken off short.*] What? Snow White alive?

THE WITCH. If these are pigs' tails, that was a pig's heart. Ask your Magic Mirror if Snow White's not alive.

THE QUEEN. [*Seizing the Mirror which hangs from her girdle.*]

> Mirror, mirror, in my hand,
> Who's the fairest in the land?

THE MIRROR. [*Answering.*]

> You, who hold me in your hand,
> You *were* fairest in the land;
> But to-day, I answer true,
> Snow White is more fair than you.

THE QUEEN. Snow White alive! [*She starts to dash the Mirror to the ground.*]

THE WITCH. [*Seizing it.*] Be careful of that Mirror, I tell you!

>'Mirror, mirror, truly tell,
>Where doth Princess Snow White dwell?

THE MIRROR. [*Answering.*]

>'Mid the ancient forest dells
>With the Seven Dwarfs she dwells.

THE WITCH. You see? Your deceitful hunts-man has let Snow White escape, and brought back a pig's heart to fool us with. Snow White has found the house of the Seven Dwarfs—and there you are, my merry lady!

THE QUEEN. The Seven Dwarfs? Who are they?

THE WITCH. Rather nice little men; sort of gnomes. Live all alone. Never saw them myself.

THE QUEEN. [*Wrapping her cloak about her.*] Where do they live?

THE WITCH. Oh, ho! Intend to deal with Snow White yourself this time, do you?

THE QUEEN. Where do they live?

THE WITCH. The usual way is about twenty miles over the mountains, but there's a short cut through my back yard. Less than a mile away.

THE QUEEN. Give me a knife or a dagger, quickly!

THE WITCH. What? Walk into the Dwarfs' house, knife in hand and crown on your head like that? *I'd* sooner dance into a hornet's nest. Really, Brangomar, if I were you I'd swap brains with a grasshopper!

THE QUEEN. But what shall I do? She's alive! She's more beautiful than I! My heart will burn itself out of my body like a live coal. Tell me some way!

THE WITCH. Deary me! Have I got to plan it all out for you again? You're a nuisance.

THE QUEEN. How? How?

[143]

THE WITCH. There's only one safe way . . .

THE QUEEN. Yes?

THE WITCH. First, I must transform you into a different looking person altogether.

THE QUEEN. And then?

THE WITCH. And then give you some means of disposing of Snow White that the Dwarfs can't trace back to you. Fiddle, fetch me the deadly poison things.

THE QUEEN. Ah, poison! Yes, that's it!
   [FIDDLE *fetches an odd looking box full of strange articles from the Magic Chest.*

THE WITCH. [*Examining them.*] Almost none left. Pair of poisoned slippers—no use. Poisoned pipe—no. Oh, here! Best thing in the box,—the poisoned apple. Beautiful, isn't it? Only the red side is poisoned, the white side is perfectly good. If you want to tempt anybody, eat the white side yourself; but the least bite of the red side, and down they drop, dead as a tombstone.

[144]

But no, you're not clever enough to be trusted with that. Ah, *here* we are,—the poisoned comb. The very thing!

THE QUEEN. Let me see it! [*She seizes the jewelled comb.*]

THE WITCH. Put that in Snow White's hair, let it stay there while you count one hundred, and all's over with her. It doesn't work instantly like the apple, but it's much safer with a stupid person like you.

THE QUEEN. How my fingers itch to set this in her black hair. Now what disguise?

THE WITCH. Disguise? Oh yes! Fiddle, bring me the Transformation Mixtures.
> [FIDDLE *brings from the chest three odd-shaped bottles, one filled with green, one with purple, and one with orange liquid.*

THE WITCH. Are these all? My entire stock of magic is running out. Lucky I'm going to retire from business next year.

THE QUEEN. [*Attempting to seize a bottle.*] Let me see . . .

THE WITCH. [*Crossly.*] Don't snatch! Wretched manners! *I'll* read the labels. [*She reads one.*] "Five drops before breakfast." Well I declare; I've written out the doses most carefully but totally forgotten what they change people into. But that's easily remedied. A drop of each in the cauldron and you'll see for yourself. Now watch!

> [*She pours a few drops from the green bottle into the cauldron. Instantly a cloud of steam rises; and in the steam—dimly at first, and then quite clearly, appears the figure of an old and wrinkled hag in threadbare garments. On one arm she carries a large basket filled with ribbons, laces, needles, thread, and such articles.*]

THE WITCH. I remember, the Old Pedlarwoman disguise. Just the thing. You could pre-

tend to be selling Snow White the comb. But let's
see what the others are, anyhow.

> [*She pours some drops from the purple bot-
> tle into the cauldron. The image of the
> Pedlar-woman vanishes; in its place ap-
> pears the figure of a small naked baby.*

THE WITCH. Oh, the baby! I used that once
myself; caught an awful cold too. Useless for you.
Now how about this orange mixture?

> [*She pours from the orange bottle. This
> time the image is that of a stout, jovial,
> red-faced man. He wears an apron and
> has a green patch over one eye. Bal-
> anced on his head he carries a tray full of
> various sorts of pies.*

THE WITCH. That's the one-eyed Pieman.
Good, but not as good as the Pedlar-woman for
your purpose.

THE QUEEN. What is a Pieman?

THE WITCH. Man who sells pies, stupid; what
did you suppose? But a Pieman wouldn't be sell-

ing combs. Pedlar-woman it is. Green bottle. [*She reads.*] "Dose, one tablespoonful, with a peppermint after." I haven't got a peppermint, but that was only to take away the taste. [*She produces a spoon and uncorks the bottle.*]

THE QUEEN. [*Hesitating.*] Is the taste very bad?

THE WITCH. Vile. Really, one of the nastiest tastes I ever made. Open your mouth.

THE QUEEN. [*Shrinking back.*] Er—is being transformed painful?

THE WITCH. No-o-o-o, but unpleasant. Feels as though you were being turned inside out like a glove. Open your mouth.

THE QUEEN. I think on the whole I'll wait till to-morrow. You see I have an important tea-party at Court this afternoon, and . . .

THE WITCH. Oh, ho! Cowardy, cowardy custard! Here, Fiddle, here's sport for you. Get the black mantle.

> [*From the chest,* FIDDLE *whisks a large black cloth embroidered with strange looking symbols, and advances toward the* QUEEN.

THE QUEEN. What is he going to do?

THE WITCH. Wrap you up so that you can't scratch while I pour this down your throat.

THE QUEEN. But I'm not ready! I must go home first!

> [*She makes a dash for the door, but* FIDDLE *is before her. Then begins a lively chase about the cave, the* QUEEN *running and dodging,* FIDDLE *following and trying to throw the black mantle over her head. The* WITCH *enjoys it all hugely, crying,* "Run, Brangomar!" "Catch her, Fiddle!" *and slapping her old knees with delight till she is quite out of breath. At last* FIDDLE *succeeds*

in cornering QUEEN BRANGOMAR, *and throws the mantle over her head.*

THE WITCH. [*Breathless.*] Well done, Fiddle, well done! Trip her up and sit on her.

> [FIDDLE *does so. The* WITCH *also sits down on the squirming* QUEEN, *and humming happily to herself pours out a tablespoonful of the green mixture.*

THE WITCH. Now, where *is* her mouth?

THE QUEEN. [*In a smothered voice.*] I won't take it! I won't!

THE WITCH. Oh, *there* it is! Thank you, Brangomar. [*She pours the dose through the cloth into the* QUEEN'S *mouth, and as the* QUEEN *writhes she goes on.*] I know it tastes bad, but nothing to make such a fuss about. [*Suddenly she holds up a warning finger.*] I feel her changing! Do you? [FIDDLE *nods.*] Done! Up with her, off with the mantle, and let's see the result.

> [FIDDLE *draws off the mantle. Lo! the* QUEEN *has been transformed into the*

[150]

likeness of the old Pedlar-woman just as it appeared in the steam, basket of goods and all.

THE WITCH. Splendid! Wouldn't recognise you myself, Brangomar. Hope you haven't lost the poisoned comb. No, here it is in your hand. Now, it wasn't half as bad as you thought it would be, was it?

THE PEDLAR-WOMAN. [*Crossly.*] It was awful! Why—is this *my* voice?

THE WITCH. Of course. Different voice with every disguise.

THE PEDLAR-WOMAN. I'm all cramps, too. How do I change back?

THE WITCH. Dear me; lucky you thought to ask. I might have forgotten. Just say:—

> "Peas porridge hot,
> "Peas porridge cold,
> "Peas porridge in the pot,
> "Nine days old;"

but say it backwards like this:

[151]

Old days nine,
Pot in the porridge peas,
Cold porridge peas,
Hot porridge peas.
That turns you right side out again.

THE PEDLAR-WOMAN. I must remember. Let me see:—"Old days nine . . ." [*But the* WITCH *claps her hand over* BRANGOMAR's *mouth.*]

THE WITCH. Gracious, woman, don't say it yet! We'd have all this to do over again. Really, you are the most senseless— Oh, be off with you. I've had quite enough of you for one day.

THE PEDLAR-WOMAN. Now for Snow White! Oh, Hex, once I set this in her hair and see her lying dead—dead before my own eyes . . .

THE WITCH. [*Interrupting.*] Don't forget to count one hundred!

THE PEDLAR-WOMAN. It will be the happiest moment of my life!

THE WITCH. Nasty disposition!

AND OFF SHE STRIDES TOWARD THE HOUSE OF THE SEVEN
DWARFS

SCENE IV

THE PEDLAR-WOMAN. [*Going to the door.*] You shan't escape me this time, my little beauty! You have no soft-hearted Berthold to deal with now, but Brangomar, Brangomar her very self! [*And off she strides toward the house of the* SEVEN DWARFS.]

> [*Left alone with* FIDDLE, *the* WITCH *goes to the blazing fire and again sits down upon it, thoughtfully.*

THE WITCH. Poor little Snow White! I'm afraid her goose is cooked this time. I'm really sorry for her. *I* don't bear her any ill will in spite of my pigs' tails. Fiddle, bring my mirror.

> [FIDDLE *brings the mirror, and* WITCH HEX *studies her new appearance carefully.*

THE WITCH. Oh, not so bad after all! They're quite becoming; sure to keep their curl in the dampest weather, and certainly the very *latest* thing!

THE CURTAIN FALLS

[153]

In the House of the Seven Dwarfs

*The room is the same as before, but quite trans-
formed by* Snow White's *house-keeping. It
shines with cleanness. There are white coverlets
on all the beds, curtains at the window, and flowers on the window-sill.* Snow White's *silver
dress has been carefully put away, and she wears
a little frock made of squirrel skins and trimmed
with bright leaves.*

It is early in the morning, and the Dwarfs *are just
starting off for the day's work. Each carries a
neat little basket of luncheon which* Snow
White *has put up, and each wears a bright bow
tie which she has made for him. They are so
proud of these ties that they have parted their
beards over their shoulders to show them.*

Snow White has just finished tying Quee's bow. She pats it into shape, kisses him, and says:

Snow White. There! Off you go!

Blick. Couldn't you please give us all another kiss?

Snow White. [*Merrily.*] No indeed!

Flick. Just one?

Snow White. Not one!

Glick. A *little* one?

Snow White. No! That's the rule: one a day, morning or night, but not both.

Blick. You see none of us ever, er—should I say "ate" or "tasted"—a kiss till you came, so perhaps we *are* a little eager about them.

Snow White. I should say you were! Why, you're perfect children about kisses and games.

[158]

SCENE V

BLICK. [*Sadly.*] That comes of our being dwarfs. You see, no dwarf is ever born till he's fifty. So, as we've never been young, we enjoy games all the more now.

SNOW WHITE. Oh, I understand, you little old dears; but still I mustn't spoil you. And that reminds me, you're not to come home any more in the middle of the morning to play games. Tuesday you came back at eleven, Wednesday at ten, and yesterday morning at nine! What sort of a way to work is that?

BLICK. [*Penitently.*] I know, but . . .

SNOW WHITE. Now not a moment before five to-day, because—[*She beckons them together and whispers.*] this is a secret—I'm going to make an enormous cake with sugar frosting for supper! Now, off with you.

BLICK. Well, brothers, ready. To-day we go into the forest for firewood. March!

[*In their usual military file the* DWARFS

march off into the forest. SNOW WHITE stands in the doorway, waving her hand after them till they are out of sight. Then with a little sigh of content she returns to the room.

SNOW WHITE. Oh, I'm so happy here. I've never been so happy in all my life. Of course I miss my dear Maids of Honour and the others; but the Dwarfs are so funny and loving and kind. [*She looks out of the window.*] It's a beautiful day. [*With a little pensive sigh.*] I wonder if I shall ever see Prince Florimond again. [*But she checks herself sharply.*] Stop that, Snow White!  You wonder about him much too often. Remember, you're not a Princess any more, only just house-keeper to the Seven Dwarfs. You must forget all about the other things. To work! Now for that cake.

[She fetches the mixing bowl. As she does so the little BROWN BIRD that guided her

*through the forest, flies to the window,
perches on the sill, and gives his call.*

SNOW WHITE. Ah, my little brown bird, back
again for your morning crumbs? Here they are.
[*She scatters the crumbs, but instead of eating
them, the little* BIRD *breaks into full song.*] Not
hungry? Just come to sing for me? You dear!
[*The song is so merry that she dances a step or
two.*] Whenever you sing, brown bird, I feel like
dancing. But I do need somebody to dance with.
The Dwarfs never can learn.

[*Just then she spies a big* WHITE BUTTER-
FLY *that is fluttering gaily by the window.*

SNOW WHITE. Oh, there's a big white butterfly. I wonder if it would come and dance with me.
[*She runs to the open door and calls.*] White
butterfly, white butterfly, will you come and
dance with Snow White? Oh, it's coming, it's coming! Sing, little brown bird! The butterfly is
coming to dance with me!

[*And indeed the* BUTTERFLY *does follow*

[161]

her into the room, and flits about here and there—now just within her grasp, now high over her head; and SNOW WHITE, *now pursuing it, now letting it follow her, does contrive a little romping dance with her new friend. And all the time the little* BROWN BIRD *sings lustily on the window sill.*

THE BUTTERFLY DANCE

SCENE V

The Butterfly Dance

Music by
Edmond Rickett. Op.25

SNOW WHITE

SCENE V

SNOW WHITE

SCENE V

[*Suddenly the* BROWN BIRD *stops singing and flies away, and the* WHITE BUTTER-FLY *darts to the door and flutters up among the tree-tops.*

SNOW WHITE. Oh, don't stop, little Bird. We want to go on. Where are you going, White Butterfly? They've both flown away! They seemed frightened.

[*She turns to see what has frightened them. The* QUEEN, *disguised as the* PEDLAR-WOMAN, *is leaning in at the window.* SNOW WHITE'S *hand springs to her heart.*

SNOW WHITE. Oh . . . !

THE PEDLAR-WOMAN. Did I frighten you, dearie? No harm in an old Pedlar-Woman.

SNOW WHITE. You *did* startle me.

THE PEDLAR-WOMAN. So that's the way you

pass your time in the forest, is it—singing and dancing? What a thing it is to be rich.

SNOW WHITE. But I'm not rich. I suppose I'm very poor now.

THE PEDLAR-WOMAN. I've come a weary way. I'm that worn and footsore . . . !

SNOW WHITE. Oh, *do* come in. I'm so sorry.

THE PEDLAR-WOMAN. [*Entering.*] Thank you, dearie. I'll just bar the door behind me for fear of the rheumatic drafts. I've been wandering days and days in this forest, and never met a soul to buy the least trinket of me.

SNOW WHITE. I'm afraid I don't think a deserted forest *is* a very good place to sell things.

THE PEDLAR-WOMAN. But *you'll* buy some little thing, my pet, some pretty little thing?

SNOW WHITE. I'm awfully sorry, but . . .

THE PEDLAR-WOMAN. Don't any of my pretty

things tempt you? And cheap!—really costs more
to sell 'em than they're worth. Look, sweetheart!

> Here's ribbons and laces,
> And gentlemen's braces,
>> A feather as white as foam;
> A chain and a locket,
> A purse for your pocket,
>> And oh, what a beautiful comb,
>>> That comb!
>> Just see, what a beautiful comb!
>
> Here's bangles and spangles,
> A bracelet with dangles,
>> A necklace with beads from Rome;
> An outfit for cross-stitch,
> The egg of an ostrich,
>> But oh, what a beautiful comb,
>>> That comb!
>> A really magnificent comb!
>
> Here's powder and patches,
> And Lucifer matches,
>> A motto with "Home, sweet Home,"
> And trimmings for frockings,

And stockings with clockings;
But nothing so fine as this comb,
This comb!
Just look, what a beautiful comb!

SNOW WHITE.   They're very attractive, but I've no money.

THE PEDLAR-WOMAN.   Now that's too bad, dearie.   I don't hardly feel as if I *could* go without leaving some little thing behind me.   Rather make you a present, so I would.

SNOW WHITE.   Oh, I couldn't take a present from you.   I ought to be giving *you* something instead.

THE PEDLAR-WOMAN.   You gave me kind words and bid me in friendly.   I'll tell you what, if you've no money I'll make you a free gift, sweetheart.

SNOW WHITE.   I couldn't really!

THE PEDLAR-WOMAN.   I'm set on it, my lamb, set on it!   Name your choice and yours it shall be.

[170]

SNOW WHITE. Well, since you're so very kind, I'll take [*she names the least valuable article*] that spool of thread.

THE PEDLAR-WOMAN. [*With pretended umbrage.*] Spool o' thread, indeed! Would you mock a poor body? Now what do you say to this comb?

SNOW WHITE. That? Why that's the *finest* thing you have.

THE PEDLAR-WOMAN. Just why I give it to you, my dear; and lovely it will look, a-shining in your black hair.

SNOW WHITE. [*Shrinking away.*] No, no! I couldn't take anything so valuable!

THE PEDLAR-WOMAN. Come, dearie, just let me put it in for you, and *then* if you don't like the look of it—well, I'll say no more and be on my way.

SNOW WHITE. I should like to see how it looks —just for fun.

THE PEDLAR-WOMAN. That's my pet; that's my sweetheart! Now sit you down, [SNOW WHITE *sits on a stool*] and shut your eyes so you shan't peep till it's in . . . are they shut?

SNOW WHITE. [*Laughing.*] Yes, tight shut!

THE PEDLAR-WOMAN. Then, here goes!
[*She puts the poisoned comb in* SNOW WHITE'S *hair. For a moment* SNOW WHITE *does not move. Then with a little moan, she rises, swaying.*

SNOW WHITE. Oh, my head—my head! [*She tries to put her hand to her head; but suddenly she totters, falls in a heap on the floor and lies quite still.*]

THE PEDLAR-WOMAN. [*Watches her for a moment, then cries exultingly.*] Ah, ha! So, my dear step-daughter, Queen Brangomar laughs last, after all! Now, to count one hundred while the poison works. [*And she begins to count.*] "One, two, three, four, five . . ." [*Suddenly she stops to listen.*] What's that?

SCENE V

[*Steps are heard outside the little house.
They come nearer. There is a knock at
the door, and* BLICK'S *voice is heard.*

BLICK. Snow White, it's us, the Dwarfs. Open
the door. [*He knocks again.*]

THE PEDLAR-WOMAN. [*In terror.*] The
Dwarfs! They'll tear me to pieces if they find me
here. I must hide her! Where, where? [*She
looks about for a place to hide* SNOW WHITE *and
seeing no other hope, drags the big table over her
and pulls the table cloth down to hide her. Meantime the* DWARFS *knock more and more impa-
tiently.*]

BLICK. Please open, Snow White. We haven't
come back for games, honestly. We want to go
down into the mines again.
       [*The* PEDLAR-WOMAN *crouches along the
       wall, looking for some means of escape.*

FLICK. [*Outside, calling.*] Snow White!

GLICK. [*Calling.*] Snow White!

ALL THE DWARFS. [*Calling together.*] Snow White!

BLICK. [*Outside.*] Brothers, there's something wrong! The window!
> [*The* DWARFS *run to the window and look in. They spy the crouching* PEDLAR-WOMAN.

PEDLAR-WOMAN. [*Realising that she is caught and ducking and curtseying.*] Oh, it's *you*, my little gentlemen!

BLICK. Open the door!

PEDLAR-WOMAN. Yes, indeed, your honours! At once, your honours! [*But as she goes to unbar the door she continues to count, under her breath.*] Twenty-one, twenty-two, twenty-three, twenty-four . . .

BLICK. [*Beating on the door.*] Quickly, I tell you!

THE PEDLAR-WOMAN. Yes, your honours!
> [*She throws the door open. The* DWARFS

---

*rush in fiercely, their little knives drawn,
and surround the* PEDLAR-WOMAN.

BLICK. What are you doing here?

FLICK. Where is Snow White?

THE PEDLAR-WOMAN. Safe and sound, my little gentlemen. But I've scarce breath to tell you. Just give me thirty seconds—or thirty-one or thirty-two or thirty-three . . .

BLICK. What are you mumbling?

THE PEDLAR-WOMAN. I was passing by with my basket o' wares . . . [BLICK *makes a threatening gesture and she hurries on with a little cry.*] . . . just passing—when your sweet little lady calls me to step in.

BLICK. Where is she now?

THE PEDLAR-WOMAN. She stepped into the forest on an errand, and bid me mind the house till she got back.

BLICK. Errand? What errand?

[175]

FLICK.   How long has she been gone?

THE PEDLAR-WOMAN.   A matter of seconds, your honour. Fifty seconds, maybe, or fifty-one or fifty-two or fifty-three or fifty-four . . .

BLICK.   [*Interrupting.*]   Well, you need stay no longer.   Go!

THE PEDLAR-WOMAN. Yes, your honours. Certainly, your honours. [*She goes courtesying to the door, but turns to say,*]   Could you tell a poor peddling body how far it might be to the next town? Is it fifty-five miles now, or fifty-six or fifty-seven or . . .

BLICK.   [*Fiercely.*]   Be off, or we'll lay hands on you!

> [*With a little scream the* PEDLAR-WOMAN *makes off; but as she passes the window she is heard still counting* "fifty-eight, fifty-nine, sixty, sixty-one . . ." *till her voice dies away in the distance.*]

BLICK.   Brothers, something's wrong!   What errand could Snow White have in the forest?

FLICK. And why didn't we meet her?

BLICK. She'd never leave the house in *her* charge.

GLICK. Unless she was frightened.

SNICK. And ran away.

FLICK. That's it!

BLICK. She may be hiding in the forest now. Quick, brothers; go east, west, north and I'll go south.

> [*All the* DWARFS *rush out except* BLICK, *who hesitates.*

BLICK. Yet it's not like Snow White to be frightened. I wonder . . . [*Suddenly he spies something on the floor near the table. It is one of* SNOW WHITE's *slippers that came off when she fell, and which the* PEDLAR-WOMAN *had overlooked.*] What's that? Her slipper! [*He calls loudly.*] Brothers, Brothers! She is here! Here is her slipper! Search the house!

> [*The* DWARFS *rush back into the room, and*

begin to seek under the beds and behind the pump; but FLICK *pulls up the table-cloth and cries:*

FLICK. Look! Here she is!
    [*They move the table away and kneel about her in consternation.*

BLICK. She has fainted. Water!

GLICK. Is she hurt?

FLICK. Unlace her bodice.

BLICK. It's loose. She's breathing, faintly.

FLICK. What's that in her hair?

BLICK. A comb. She never wore it before. Out with it! [*He draws the comb from* SNOW WHITE'S *hair; but suddenly hurls it away, crying.*] Oh! it burned my fingers!

SNICK. Poisoned?

GLICK. Look!
    [SNOW WHITE'S *eyelids flutter and she sighs.*

THEY KNEEL ABOUT HER IN CONSTERNATION

BLICK. See! her eyes! She's coming to!

[SNOW WHITE *stirs; then opens her eyes and lifts her head.*

SNOW WHITE. Oh . . . what . . . what happened?

THE DWARFS. [*Tenderly.*] Snow White!

SNOW WHITE. I was talking with the old Pedlar-woman . . .

BLICK. Ah! the old woman!

SNOW WHITE. And . . . where is she? Why, there's the comb!

BLICK. The comb?

SNOW WHITE. She wanted to give it to me. I let her put it in my hair just to see how it looked and then I must have fainted.

BLICK. Brothers, that comb *was* poisoned.

FLICK. She tried to poison our Snow White.

SNOW WHITE. To poison me? Perhaps it *may*

[179]

have been the comb. But she didn't. You saved me, didn't you, my dear brothers. I'm all alive again! And quite well! See? [*She rises.*]

BLICK. [*Ominously.*] Brothers! [*He draws his knife, and the others follow his example.*] Snick, you stay to guard Snow White. The rest follow me.

[*They hasten toward the door.*

SNOW WHITE. [*Stopping them.*] Where are you going?

BLICK. [*Terribly.*] To catch that Pedlar-woman.

SNOW WHITE. Oh, please don't! Why should *she* want to poison me? The only one who might want to harm me is Queen Brangomar.

BLICK. Snow White, I believe *that* was Queen Brangomar.

SNOW WHITE. Oh, no! Brangomar is very beautiful.

BLICK. But she knows magic; she may have disguised herself. Come, brothers!

SNOW WHITE. [*Barring the way.*] Oh, please, please don't go. She might harm you!

BLICK. [*Scornfully.*] Harm us! Let me go, Snow White.

SNOW WHITE. [*Clinging to him.*] No, no! Listen! If that *was* Brangomar she'll think I'm all dead now and won't try again; but if she finds out that I am still alive, she might. Don't you see?

BLICK. [*Hesitating.*] I see,—but . . .

SNOW WHITE. Oh, I ask you, *please!*

BLICK. It's not fair to ask us "*please.*"

SNOW WHITE. But I do. I ask you please, please, *please!*

BLICK. [*As he sheathes his knife.*] Well—this
[181]

time. But, brothers, we must guard our Princess more carefully in future.

THE DWARFS. Yes, indeed!

BLICK. Snow White, promise that when we're away you will keep the door barred, and never let any one in.

GLICK. No matter who they are.

FLICK. No matter *what* they look like.

SNOW WHITE. Oh, I'm not afraid!

BLICK. But you must promise, solemnly.

SNOW WHITE. Oh, very well, I promise—

"Truly, rooly,
"Black and bluely,
"Cross my heart!"

Now, let's forget all about such disagreeable things. To celebrate—[*She claps her hands.*] I'll tell you, let's declare this morning a holiday!

THE DWARFS. [*Dancing with delight.*] A holiday?

SNOW WHITE. And we'll all play a game before you go back to the mines.

THE DWARFS. Hip, hip, hurrah!

SNOW WHITE. Shall we play "Blind Man's Buff" or "Puss-in-the-Corner" or "Snap the Whip"?

THE DWARFS. [*Chanting in chorus.*] "Blind Man's Buff," "Puss-in-the-Corner" AND "Snap the Whip"!

SNOW WHITE. All three? Well, "Blind Man's Buff" first.

BLICK. Clear away!

> *They clear the floor for Games, and begin with "Blind Man's Buff." The* DWARFS *always want* SNOW WHITE *to choose who shall be blind-folded—they never can agree among themselves—and she chooses* GLICK. *Now,* GLICK *is a very spry old fellow, and he nearly catches* WHICK *on the very first dash; so nearly*

[183]

that WHICK *only escapes by crawling under a bed. Next, he corners* QUEE; *but* QUEE *is so small that he creeps out between* GLICK'S *legs. It is a long while before* GLICK *can touch anybody else; and indeed he only catches* SNICK *at last because* SNICK *trips over his own long beard, and falls flat. Even then it takes* GLICK *some time to tell whom he has caught, for the* DWARFS *are all very much alike. But at last* GLICK *feels a bump on* SNICK'S *bald head that came at least a hundred and twenty-five years ago when an enormous diamond fell on him in the mines, and has never gone away again.*

Next they play, "Puss-in-the-Corner," and get so excited about it that they clamber all over the clean, starched coverlets that SNOW WHITE *had only just finished ironing; so she is relieved when the game is over.*

Finally comes "Snap-the-Whip." They

[184]

*"snap" it so hard that when the line
breaks they all fall down, puffing and
holding their old sides; and little* QUEE,
*the "snapper," has to turn four complete
somersaults before he can stop.*

*No sooner have they got breath again
than they all surround* SNOW WHITE,
*dancing up and down, and crying:
"More, more, more!" But she shakes
her head firmly.*

SNOW WHITE. Dear me, no! Remember, I
have that cake to bake before supper. You really
must go. And don't come back till five.

FLICK. Oh, please make it four.

SNICK. Or half past, anyhow.

SNOW WHITE. No, five. Not a moment sooner.

BLICK. [*Resignedly.*] Well, brothers, march.
[*And down they all file into the underground passage leaving* SNOW WHITE
alone.]

[185]

SNOW WHITE. Hasn't this been a morning! I only got as far with that cake as the bowl. Now, first the flour. [*She puts some flour in the bowl, and then suddenly remembers.*] Gracious! I almost forgot my promise to bar the door!

> [*She bars the door; but as she does so she hears, in the forest, a distant sort of chanting song. It comes nearer.*

SNOW WHITE. What's that? Somebody singing? I was only just in time. Why, they're coming here!

> [*You can hear the words of the chanting clearly now. They are:*

> Anybody want to buy,
> Any sort of baker's pie?
> Pies! Pies! Pies! Pies!

SNOW WHITE. Oh, a baker-man selling pies. Really, people do have the most curious ideas about this forest.

> [*The person coming is, as a matter of fact,* QUEEN BRANGOMAR *in another disguise.*
> [186]

She suspected that the DWARFS *might take the comb from* SNOW WHITE'S *hair before the poison had time to do its work; so she hastened back to the* WITCH— *who wasn't a bit glad to see her—and with a dose from the orange bottle transformed herself again, this time into the likeness of the One-eyed Pieman. Then she—or I suppose I should say he— hastened back to the forest, and now, after spying about to make sure that the* DWARFS *are not near, has approached the house with the tray of pies on his head.*

THE PIEMAN. [*Close behind the door now.*]

Anybody want to buy,
Any sort of baker's pie?
Pies! Pies! Pies! Pies! Pies!

[*He knocks at the door, "rat-a-tat-tat; tat-tat."* SNOW WHITE *does not answer. The* PIEMAN *goes to the window and looks in.*

THE PIEMAN. Hello! Didn't you hear me knock?

SNOW WHITE. I'm sorry, but I can't let you in.

THE PIEMAN. Oh, cooking, I see. Just ready to mix, eh? That's my line of business; baker— pies, all kinds. [*He chants rapidly.*]

Pumpkin, custard, veal-and-ham,
Chocolate, lemon, squash and lamb,
Gooseberry, blueberry, peach and quince,
Chicken, cocoanut, apple, mince.

SNOW WHITE. I really don't want any, thank you.

THE PIEMAN. Of course not. No good cook would ever eat a baker's pie; and you *are* a good cook.

SNOW WHITE. [*A little flattered.*] Well, I've had some experience.

THE PIEMAN. I can tell that by the hitch of your apron. Now my specialty is apple pies, and . . .

[188]

SNOW WHITE. [*Interrupting.*] Oh, please don't offer to give me one. I couldn't take it.

THE PIEMAN. Who was offering? I just wanted to ask your opinion.

SNOW WHITE. [*Contritely.*] I beg your pardon. Of course I'll give you my opinion.

THE PIEMAN. You know that old apple tree half a mile back? Do those apples make good pies?

SNOW WHITE. I don't know.

THE PIEMAN. They look splendid. Here's one I picked. It's as red and white as your face. If it is a good pie apple, I'll go back and get a sackful.

SNOW WHITE. You can't tell from the looks, you know. Some are too sweet and some are too sour.

THE PIEMAN. Well, taste, and we'll compare opinions. You eat the red half and I'll eat the white. [*He splits the apple in two, and tosses the*

[189]

red half through the window into SNOW WHITE'S *apron.*] Catch! [*He eats his half.*] Just right to me, sweet *and* sour.

SNOW WHITE. [*Starts to taste her half; but then, with a faint suspicion, she sets it down and says:*] Thank you, but I don't eat between meals.

THE PIEMAN. [*Munching luxuriously.*] What, temper touchy? Well, I don't blame you. Often feel like that myself on baking days. But this tastes to me like a prime pie apple. I advise you to get some. Luck to your baking! Goodday. [*Repeating his cry.*]

> Anybody want to buy,
> Any sort of baker's pie,
> > Pies! Pies! Pies! Pies! Pies!
> > > [*He makes off into the forest.*

SNOW WHITE. [*Alone and penitently.*] I was horrid to him. He only wanted my advice. He didn't try to come in. It *is* a splendid apple. [*She looks at it longingly.*] If it's good I could make

[190]

the Dwarfs an apple-dumpling apiece. He ate his half.

> [*She bites the red cheek of the apple. Suddenly she grasps her throat, whirls about once, falls, and lies quite still. After a moment, the face of the* PIEMAN *appears at the window, peering in cautiously.*]

THE PIEMAN. Ah, she *did* taste it! I thought she would if I went away. But there must be no mistake this time. No more mistakes! [*He leans through the window, and with his staff pries up the bar that fastens the door.*] First, off with this disguise. [*He repeats:*]

> Old days nine,
> Pot in the porridge peas,
> Cold porridge peas,
> Hot porridge peas.

> [*And instantly the* PIEMAN's *outward appearance changes, and it is* QUEEN BRANGOMAR *in her royal robes that*

sweeps into the room and hastens to
SNOW WHITE's body.

THE QUEEN. [Kneeling beside SNOW WHITE.]
No breath! No heart! Quite dead at last! This
time, my lady, white as snow, red as blood and
black as ebony the Dwarfs cannot wake you. But
I must hide that. [She picks up the apple.] They
mustn't trace me. [Then rising she strides to the
door and cries:] Now, you wretched little dwarfs,
you miserable little gnomes, you moles, you earth-
worms, bring her to life this time if you can. I defy
you! Queen Brangomar defies you! [She rushes
off into the wood crying as she goes:] Dead at
last! At last! At last!

> [Hardly has the QUEEN's voice died
> away, when the stone over the un-
> derground passage is lifted, and
> BLICK appears.

> BLICK. [Anxiously.] Did you
> call, Snow White? I was standing
> guard, and I thought I heard . . .

[He sees SNOW WHITE's prostrate body. He goes

"AH, SHE DID TASTE IT! I THOUGHT SHE WOULD IF I WENT AWAY"

to her and touches her hand. It is cold. With a voice of agony, he cries down the passage:] Brothers! Brothers!

THE CURTAIN FALLS

[*After a moment it rises again. It is moonlight now; and the* DWARFS, *with lighted lanterns are grouped about the bed on which they have laid* SNOW WHITE. *All day long they have tried to restore her. They have bathed her face with water and wine, and fanned her, and chafed her little hands and feet, but without avail. After a long silence* BLICK *speaks.*

BLICK. There is no hope, my brothers. There is nothing more to do. Our Snow White is dead.

[*One by one they kneel about her, silently; but little* QUEE, *unable to restrain his tears, falls sobbing at her feet.*

AGAIN THE CURTAIN FALLS

Scene VI

A Glade in the Deep Wood

The Dwarfs *have laid* Snow White *in a coffin
made all of clear crystal and wrought silver, and
set it in this secret glade. The glade is near to
their house, but so encircled by great trees as to
be hidden from every side. Here for nearly a
year they have watched over her, day and night,
two watching at a time. Every morning they
weave a fresh pall of ferns and wild flowers to
lay over the coffin when the sun has risen high;
and so covered it looks like a ferny mound blos-
soming.*

To-night Snick *and* Flick *are on watch. They
sit silent for a time.*

Snick.   The moon has been up an hour.

FLICK. It is time Blick came to take my place.

SNICK. I wish it were always my turn to watch. I have no heart for anything else.

FLICK. Nor I, brother, nor I!

SNICK. Here comes Blick now.

FLICK. Why is he running?
[BLICK *enters breathless.*

BLICK. Danger! Put out your lanterns! A man has been prowling about the forest since sundown. He is ragged and wild and carries a knife. We have surrounded him; we will pounce out and bind him; but he looks strong. We shall need you, Snick. Flick must guard alone. Come this way, but keep behind the trees. The others are closing in.
[*They creep off.* FLICK, *left alone, covers the coffin with the pall, and then goes to the edge of the glade.*

[198]

FLICK. Ah, I see him. He has come out into the open. They are stealing up behind him. He sees them! his knife is out! Quick, quick, brothers! They have him now. Down he goes like a falling tree. Bind him fast, brothers! [*He shouts.*] This way! This way!

> [*Presently the other* DWARFS *drag the strange man to the spot. They have bound him with many ropes. His clothes are ragged and he looks unkempt and wild. It is* BERTHOLD *the Huntsman.*

BLICK. Let him get up, but take away his knife.
> [*They wrest* BERTHOLD's *knife from him. He staggers to his feet.*

BERTHOLD. What is all this? The first I know I am on my back and bound. Who are you that are so little and so strong?

BLICK. We are the Seven Dwarfs of this Forest. What are you doing in our domain?

BERTHOLD. Dwarfs? I mean you no harm.

BLICK. What are you doing here?

BERTHOLD. I am seeking some one who was lost here—lost long ago; but I must search every inch of this wood. Let me go.

BLICK. Tell us who you are.

BERTHOLD. No!

BLICK. We shall keep you prisoner till you do.

BERTHOLD. I cannot tell you.

BLICK. Bind him to a tree till he is ready to speak.

BERTHOLD. No, no, let me go! I must search all night. I must not lose a moment. If I tell you why I am searching will you let me go?

BLICK. We make no promises.

BERTHOLD. You have good faces; I will trust you. A year ago in this forest I—left—a young girl. I cannot tell you why, but oh, I thought it wise at the time. I was to come back next day and care for her; but when I reached the city I was seized and imprisoned.

FLICK. [*Crying out.*] Can *he* be . . . ?

BLICK. Hush! [*To* BERTHOLD.] Go on!

BERTHOLD. It has taken me a whole year to escape. I dug a tunnel under the prison tower with that broken knife. I first saw daylight yesterday. I stopped only to hide my children; then I fled here to the forest to search. I have little hope—how could she live a year?—but I must search! Now, will you let me go?

> [*There is a moment's silence.* BLICK *consults the others with a look, and replies.*

BLICK. If you can answer three questions we will let you go.

BERTHOLD. [*Wonderingly.*] Questions?

BLICK. Who was the woman who imprisoned you?

BERTHOLD. Woman? How did you know

that? It *was* a woman, and the wickedest on this earth—Queen Brangomar!

BLICK. Your name is—Berthold?

BERTHOLD. [*Amazed.*] You know me?

BLICK. [*Softly.*] Who was the—child?

BERTHOLD. Her name was Snow White.

BLICK. [*Gently.*] Loose him, brothers.
    [*Quickly the* DWARFS *strip the ropes from*
        BERTHOLD'S *arms; but he cries out.*

BERTHOLD. No, no, do not stop for that! Do you know anything of her? Tell me in pity's name. Is she alive?

BLICK. Alas, poor Berthold, one look will tell you more than many words. Brothers, uncover her.
      [*Reverently two of the* DWARFS *strip*
        back the pall from the coffin and reveal
        SNOW WHITE. *Her little silver dress*

gleams in the moonlight. She looks as
fair as if she had just fallen asleep.
[*With a cry* BERTHOLD *sinks on his knees*
beside her.

BERTHOLD. Snow White! Oh my Princess! Dead! I knew it must be so; but I hoped against hope!

WHICK. [*Gently.*] She wandered to us in the Forest. She lived with us. We cared for her.

BLICK. Once before she was in peril, and we saved her; but this time we came too late.

BERTHOLD. When did it happen,—yesterday?

BLICK. No, many months ago. But her red lips have never paled, nor her white skin looked less fair than snow. We could not bear to hide her away in the black earth, so we made this coffin of crystal and silver, and wrote her name upon it, "The Princess Snow White." And here we watch over her night and day. We loved her so!

BERTHOLD.   You could not love her more than I.   [*His head sinks on his arms and he sobs.*]

[*With a quick gesture* BLICK *gathers the* DWARFS *about him, and whispers to them.*

BLICK.   Brothers, he loved her, and he is a *man!* Let us ask what he would do.

THE DWARFS.   [*In eager whispers.*] Yes! Yes!

[BLICK *gently replaces the pall.*

BERTHOLD.   No, no, do not cover her!   Let me look at her always.

BLICK. Berthold, is it enough to watch? Month after month, *we* have watched, but we are Dwarfs.   We thought a *Man* would not be satisfied to weep.

BERTHOLD.   [*Rising.*]   You do well to rouse me.   She shall be avenged!

[*The* DWARFS *look at one another their*

eyes burning with excitement; but BLICK *goes on quietly.*

BLICK. Ah, that is what we have longed to do—how we have longed!

BERTHOLD. But you have done nothing?

BLICK. What could we do? [*He bows his head.*] We are Dwarfs. We know nothing of the world of men and cities. We hoped that her enemy might some day creep back here. But we are not even sure who . . .

BERTHOLD. Sure? It was Brangomar, the only enemy our little Princess ever had.

BLICK. And Brangomar is—a Queen!

SNICK. Upon a Throne!

GLICK. With a great Court about her!

FLICK. In a great City!

WHICK. Full of tall people!

BLICK. [*Bursting out with passionate eager-*

ness.] But oh, do not think we are *afraid*. No! We will follow if you will but lead us. Say you will lead us, Berthold!

BERTHOLD. I will lead you. You are my brothers now.

BLICK. You know the way?

BERTHOLD. Like my name.

BLICK. Is it very far?

BERTHOLD. It we journey all night we shall see the city walls by noon.

FLICK. How many people make a city?

SNICK. Shall we fight all the court?

BLICK. Will they—will they laugh at us?

BERTHOLD. [*Fiercely.*] Laugh? Not for long! The people love her even as we do. You shall bear her on your shoulders. When they see her they will rise to avenge her! And, to the Queen—death!

THE DWARFS. [*Solemnly.*] Death!

BERTHOLD. We will enter the city crying, "In the name of our Princess Snow White!"

THE DWARFS. [*Repeating solemnly.*] "In the name of our Princess Snow White!"

BERTHOLD. Lift her up and come.

> [*Gently the* DWARFS *raise* SNOW WHITE'S *coffin on their shoulders, and following* BERTHOLD, *march out of the moonlit glade and into the deep shadow of the Forest on their way to the City as*

THE CURTAIN FALLS

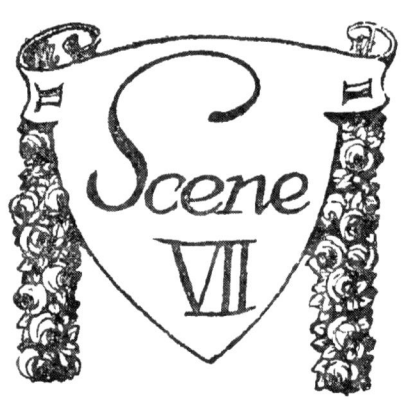

Scene

VII

The Throne Room of the Palace

Sir Dandiprat *is standing in the middle of the room, surrounded by all the* Maids of Honour. *He looks puzzled and distressed.*

Rosalys.   [*To* Sir Dandiprat.]   Of course it's to-day that Snow White is coming home.

Amelotte.   It's a year and a day to-day.

Christabel.   We thought of course you knew.

Sir Dandiprat.   Dear me; are you sure?   It's most important.

Christabel.   She went away to school on the twentieth of June.

Rosalys.   Last year.

ASTOLAINE. And to-day is the twenty-first.

ROSALYS. This year.

CHRISTABEL. So it must be a year and a day to-day.

SIR DANDIPRAT. Pooh, that's not the way to reckon it. It ought to be done by arithmetic. Let me see— [*He shuts his eyes and repeats.*]
"Thirty days hath September,
"April, June and . . ."

CHRISTABEL. [*Interrupting.*] That's no use!

SIR DANDIPRAT. Oh, I know—I know now! How many days are there in a year.

ROSALYS. [*Hiding a smile.*] Three hundred and sixty-five usually.

SIR DANDIPRAT. I've got it now! Quiet! Quiet! I take June twentieth, [*He writes on his tablet with his big gold pencil.*] and add three hundred and sixty-five. She ought to arrive on June

[212]

the three-hundred-and-eighty-fifth. Hm—that can't be right. It's most puzzling.

ROSALYS. Prince Florimond comes to-day too.

SIR DANDIPRAT. What? Prince Florimond *too?*

ASTOLAINE. Of course—to be engaged to Snow White.

SIR DANDIPRAT. The Prince coming and nothing arranged—nothing! Nobody ever tells me anything at this Court. He may be here any moment, and all the army out hunting for Berthold, and the Dukes and Duchesses scattered all over the place playing croquet! I shall go distracted! I shall go distracted!

> [*He hurries out onto the terrace, and first turns to the right, then to the left, then to the right again, before he can finally make up his foolish old mind to go the left, and waddles out of sight.*

CHRISTABEL. I hope Snow White will come before the Prince does.

GUINIVERE. I shall hug her to death.

ASTOLAINE. I didn't really believe a year and a day would *ever* be over.

ROSALYS. Just think how much she'll know.

 CHRISTABEL. I hope she'll know more than the Queen.

ASTOLAINE. And asks questions the Queen can't answer.

ERMENGARDE. Wouldn't that be fun!

CHRISTABEL. Oh, let's play that Snow White is coming home. I'll be Snow White . . .

GUINIVERE. You always want to be Snow White.

CHRISTABEL. [*Ignoring the interruption, to* ASTOLAINE.] You be the Queen. [*To* ROSALYS.] You be the Prince.

AMELOTTE. I'll be Sir Dandiprat.

[214]

HERE FOR NEARLY A YEAR THEY HAVE WATCHED OVER HER, DAY
AND NIGHT

CHRISTABEL. Well then, announce the Prince. [*And she and* ROSALYS *run out onto the terrace ready to re-enter as* SNOW WHITE *and the* PRINCE *respectively.*]

ASTOLAINE. Wait till I get on the throne. [*She arranges an imaginary train, then sweeps to the throne and gazes into an imaginary mirror.*] I think I'm looking particularly handsome to-day. Any visitors, Sir Dandiprat?

AMELOTTE. [*As* SIR DANDIPRAT, *announcing.*] His Royalty Prince Florimond, your Majesty.
[ROSALYS *enters as the* PRINCE, *bowing low in the doorway.*

ROSALYS. Has Princess Snow White come home yet, your Majesty? I love her to distractedness. I should like to marry her at once, please.

CHRISTABEL. [*Peeping in from the terrace.*] Now me.

ASTOLAINE. No, wait! Let me talk a *little.* Dear me, Prince Florimond—I mean, dear us!—we

don't understand what you can possibly see in that
plain child . . .

> [*But* CHRISTABEL *will wait no longer, and
> appears in the doorway.*

AMELOTTE. [*Pushing her back.*] Wait till I
announce you. [*Resuming* SIR DANDIPRAT'S
voice.] Here's the Princess now. Most important. The Princess Snow White.

> [CHRISTABEL *re-enters, makes a curtsey as
> much like* SNOW WHITE'S *as she can;
> then going to* PRINCE ROSALYS, *she says:*

CHRISTABEL. You ought to speak
first.

ROSALYS. [*As the* PRINCE, *kneeling.*] Snow White, I love you very
much. May I kiss your hand?

CHRISTABEL. [*As* SNOW WHITE.] I should be
very much obliged. Now I should like to ask the
Queen something. Can your Majesty spell "hip-
popotamus?" [*She adds hastily.*] You mustn't
be able to.

ASTOLAINE. [*Indignantly.*] I wasn't going to!
[*Then, as the* QUEEN *again, and in a loud whisper.*] However do you spell it, Sir Dandiprat?

AMELOTTE. [*As* SIR DANDIPRAT.] I can't
think, your Majesty.

ASTOLAINE. You never do!

AMELOTTE. [*Strutting about with puffed out
cheeks.*] Really I shall go distracted! I shall go
dis . . . [*But she has to clap her hand quickly over
her mouth for the real* SIR DANDIPRAT'S *voice is
heard on the terrace, exclaiming,* "Really, I shall
go distracted!"; *and in he bustles, followed by all
the* DUKES *and* DUCHESSES, *whom he hastily arranges in their proper places about the room.*]

SIR DANDIPRAT. The Prince is here! The
Prince is here! We're keeping his Highness waiting! Quickly, quickly, my dear Dukes and Duchesses. Quickly, quickly!

> [*A trumpet sounds, and* PRINCE FLORI-
> MOND *enters, followed by his* PAGES.
> *The* COURTIERS *bow low.*

SIR DANDIPRAT. I'm sorry to have kept your Highness waiting. I'll inform the Queen at once that you've arrived. She's been expecting you all the morning. Just a moment, your Highness. [*As he makes for the door he whispers to* CHRISTA-BEL.] Where is the Queen?

CHRISTABEL. Try in front of all the looking-glasses!

SIR DANDIPRAT. [*Shocked.*] Most disrespect-ful! You will drive me distracted—distracted! [*He paddles off to find the* QUEEN.]

THE PRINCE. [*To* ROSALYS.] Lady Rosalys, has the Princess returned?

ROSALYS. [*Curtseying.*] Not yet, your High-ness, but we expect her every moment.

THE PRINCE. Is she well?

ROSALYS. I don't know, your Highness. She hasn't written to us since she went away.

THE PRINCE. Not a single letter?
[SIR DANDIPRAT *reappears and announces.*

[218]

Sir Dandiprat. Her Majesty, the Queen.

> [Queen Brangomar *enters, and with a
> haughty nod to* Prince Florimond,
> *sweeps to the throne.*

The Queen. I totally forgot you were coming
to-day, Florimond. Stupid of me. Poor boy, I've
sad news for you. I ought to have written but I
hated to distress you. It's about Snow White.

The Prince. Snow White!

The Queen. I deeply regret to say she is dead.

The Prince. Dead . . . !

The Queen. It happened at boarding-school a
few days after she arrived.

The Prince. [*Crying out.*] Snow White
. . . dead . . . !

The Queen. I sent at least eighteen doctors,
but it was useless.

> [*The* Prince *sinks sobbing on the steps of
> the throne.*

THE QUEEN. Pray don't distress yourself. Everything possible has been done. I built a splendid monument over her grave; a tall gilded shaft surrounded by four groups of ... [*Suddenly she sees the stern figure of* BERTHOLD. *He has been standing silent and unnoticed in the doorway. She cries out.*] Berthold!

BERTHOLD. [*Advancing.*] Yes, Berthold! Berthold, come to punish you!

THE QUEEN. Seize him! Arrest him! Dandiprat, the soldiers!

SIR DANDIPRAT. I'm awfully sorry, your Majesty, but the soldiers are all out hunting for him!

BERTHOLD. I fear neither your soldiers nor your witchcraft now. No army, no Court, no Kingdom will be yours when I have told my tale.

THE QUEEN. [*Shrieking.*] Don't listen to him! He is mad! I imprisoned him because he was mad.

BERTHOLD. No, for fear that I would reveal

your wickedness. But I escaped. I tunnelled under the tower and fled back to the forest to search for Snow White. Last night, in a secret dell, I found . . . [*His voice falters.*]

THE PRINCE. [*Rising with a cry.*] You found her?

BERTHOLD. Yes. But she lay in a coffin all made of shining crystal, as fair as if she were but asleep. And guarding her, day and night, were Seven Dwarfs.

THE QUEEN. But she is dead?

BERTHOLD. Yes, and you did the deed.

THE QUEEN. [*Trying to regain her self-control.*] Nonsense! The man is quite mad. Snow White died at boarding-school. I made the arrangements myself.

BERTHOLD. With that falsehood on your lips, —look!

> [*The* SEVEN DWARFS *appear on the terrace bearing* SNOW WHITE'S *coffin cov-*

*ered with its pall of flowers. They
march slowly into the room.*

THE QUEEN. [*Cowering on her throne in an
agony of fear.*] The Dwarfs! Merciful stars,
what are they bringing? No! No! Take it away,
take it away! You shall not bring her here! You
shall not!

> [*Rushing from the throne, the* QUEEN
> *hurls herself upon the* DWARFS *to pre-
> vent their setting down the coffin. So
> sudden is her onslaught that they cannot
> resist her; and with a crash of crystal it
> is overturned. With a cry of horror the*
> DWARFS *surround it, and the* COURTIERS
> *crowd about them.*
>
> [*For a moment the* QUEEN *is alone. She
> seizes the Magic Mirror that hangs at
> her girdle, and with trembling lips whis-
> pers.*

THE QUEEN.

> Mirror, Mirror, in my hand,
> Who's the fairest in the land?

SCENE VII

[*What the Mirror answers will never be known for hardly has it begun to speak when, with a cry of rage, the* QUEEN *dashes it into a thousand pieces on the floor. Suddenly she clasps her hands over her face, sinks to her knees with a moan, and draws her veil close.*

[*And now there is a gasp of wonder from the* COURTIERS, *and* ROSALYS' *voice cries.*

ROSALYS. Oh, look! Snow White!
　　[*The group parts, and* SNOW WHITE, *half supported by the* DWARFS, *is seen to stir.*

THE PRINCE. [*Rushing to her.*] Snow White! My beloved! She lives! [*He kneels beside her and raises her head.*]

SNOW WHITE. [*With a deep sigh.*] Oh it was such a long, sad dream. I dreamed that I was dead. It was all dark and still. I could not move or see. Then, just now, came that great noise,—was it an earthquake?—and this loosened in my throat. Why, see, it's a little piece of apple! Then there was a warm rushing here. [*She lays her hand on her breast.*] and I woke up. Or am I dreaming now? No, there are my Dwarfs. And Rosalys and Christabel and . . . Where am I? [*With a cry of fear she struggles to her feet.*] This is the palace! The Queen will find me! Hide me, brothers, I'm afraid!

BERTHOLD. [*Pouncing upon the cowering* QUEEN.] She shall never harm you again, my Princess! What shall her punishment be? Let us starve her in the Grey Tower as she would have starved my children.

BLICK. I'll make her a pair of red hot iron shoes to dance in at your wedding.

DANDIPRAT. If I might suggest, your Highness . . .

> [*But the* QUEEN, *writhing from* BER-
> THOLD'S *grasp, creeps to* SNOW WHITE'S
> *feet, and makes an imploring gesture.*

SNOW WHITE. Hush, please, I think she wants to speak to me.

THE QUEEN. [*Whispering.*] Yes, to you alone.

SNOW WHITE. She wants to speak to me alone. Please let her.

BERTHOLD. Be careful, Princess!

SNOW WHITE. I'm not afraid any more. Leave us for a moment.
[*The others withdraw a little, leaving* SNOW WHITE *and the* QUEEN *together.*

THE QUEEN. [*In a muffled voice.*] Oh, Snow White, my punishment has come! I broke the Mirror, and my beauty is gone forever!

SNOW WHITE. The Mirror?

THE QUEEN. Oh, forgive me. I shall never be jealous of you again. Only let me go away where no one can ever see my face. You shall be Queen now. Here is the Crown. [*She thrusts it into* SNOW WHITE's hand.]

SNOW WHITE. [*Wonderingly.*] I to be Queen? I don't understand.

THE QUEEN. You don't believe me? Then, look,—but, oh let no one else see me! [*She lifts her veil a little so that* SNOW WHITE *alone can see her face.*]

SNOW WHITE. Oh, how dreadful! Poor Brangomar! I forgive you, I pity you from the bottom of my heart! [*She turns to the others.*] Please let the Queen go away unharmed. She wants to go far, far away.

BERTHOLD. [*Barring the way.*] Unpunished? Never, your Highness!

ALL. Never, never!

SNOW WHITE. I beseech you. She will never harm any one again. I answer for her. I have forgiven her. Let her go.

> [*Reluctantly the* COURTIERS *part and make a way for the* QUEEN. *She kisses the hem of* SNOW WHITE'S *dress; and*

*then, her veil drawn close, makes her
way toward the door.*

[*But just as she reaches the terrace who
should appear there but* WITCH HEX.
*She looks very differently now. In-
stead of her red cloak and pointed hat
she wears a neat black silk dress with a
white fichu around her shoulders, and a
black bonnet with lavender-coloured
flowers. On her arm she carries a basket
in which is an ordinary sized black cat.*

THE WITCH. [*Stopping the* QUEEN.] High-
ty-tighty, what's all this?

THE QUEEN. [*Clinging to her.*] Oh, Witch
Hex!

ALL. [*In consternation.*] Witch Hex! The
Witch!

THE WITCH. Don't be frightened; not *Witch*
Hex any more! I gave up magic for good and all
day before yesterday, burned all my charms, shrunk
Fiddle to his natural size, [*She shows the cat.*] and

[227]

retired. Perfectly respectable old lady now. But whatever have you been doing to Brangomar?

THE QUEEN. Oh, Hex, I broke the Magic Mirror.

THE WITCH. And turned ugly. I told you you would some day. Well, serves you right. Let's see. [*She tries to lift the* QUEEN's *veil.*]

THE QUEEN. [*Preventing her.*] Oh, no, no, no!

THE WITCH. Oh, yes, yes, yes! You were fond enough of showing your face before. Turn about's fair play. [*She snatches off the veil.*]
> [*The* QUEEN *has surely turned ugly, but it is a funny kind of ugliness. None of her features have changed except her nose, but that has grown enormous—almost a foot long, and very red.*

THE WITCH. [*Cackling with laughter.*] Oh my stars and garters! What a nose! What a nose!

SNOW WHITE. [*Appealingly.*] Please don't laugh at her!

THE QUEEN. Oh, Hex, can't you help me?

THE WITCH. Afraid not. The only way to be beautiful without magic is to be good. Who are all these fine folks?

SIR DANDIPRAT. [*Strutting forward importantly.*] Allow me to present . . .

THE WITCH. [*Waving him away.*] Shoo, shoo! old turkey-cock!
> [*Meantime the* QUEEN *creeps quietly away on the terrace, and is never seen or heard of again.*]

THE WITCH. [*Going to* SNOW WHITE.] You must be Snow White. However did you come alive? I made a poisoned apple for you. Glad it didn't work, but why didn't it?

SNOW WHITE. [*Smiling.*] I think the big greedy bite I took must have stuck in my throat;

and just now something happened, and it got jog-gled out.

THE WITCH. Glad of it. Always was sorry for you. Who's this nice boy? Oh, Prince Flori-mond of course. I can guess why *you're* here. Well, is the betrothal all arranged? [SNOW WHITE *hangs her head, and the* PRINCE *blushes furiously.*] Embarrassed, eh? Well, I don't know of any better use for bold old people than to help shy young people. Where's the ring, young man? Oh, come! I'll wager you've been carry-ing it about for a year. [*Shyly* PRINCE FLORI-MOND *produces the ring.*] Your hand, Snow White!

SNOW WHITE. Please, do you think I ought to —yet? You see I didn't get to school to be pre-pared and . . .

THE WITCH. You're just a dear sweet little girl, and that's good enough for any man, prince or pauper. Put it on, Florimond. [*The* PRINCE *does so.*] Now, young man, lead her to the throne

[230]

and crown her properly, and we'll all swear allegiance to our new little Queen.

> [*With stately grace the young* PRINCE *leads* SNOW WHITE *to the throne, and reverently sets the great crown on her little head. Then he kneels before her, and all the* COURTIERS *follow his example. Then there is a great burst of music and all the trumpets in the palace blare. Rising and unsheathing his sword, the* PRINCE *cries.*

THE PRINCE. Love and homage to our little Queen!

ALL. [*In a great shout.*] Love and homage to our little Queen!

SNOW WHITE. [*Furtively brushing away a happy tear.*] Oh please . . . please!

> [*During all this the* DWARFS *have withdrawn shyly to the furthest corner of the room; but now* BLICK, *clearing his throat and summoning all his courage, cries:*

BLICK. Brothers! March!

> [*In military order the* DWARFS *file to the
> throne. Some of them think they ought
> to kneel, and some of them think not, so
> they wobble for a moment and then
> stand still.*

BLICK. [*Stammering.*] Your er . . . er . . .
your . . . [*He gives it up, and bursts out.*] Oh
Snow White, please tell us what to call you? You
see we've never met a Queen before.

SNOW WHITE. Oh my brothers, call me just
Snow White—always and always!

BLICK. Snow White, may we go now?

SNOW WHITE. Go? Where?

BLICK. To fetch you our wedding present—all
our gold and jewels. We'll make you the richest
Queen in the whole world.

SNICK. And then back to our lonely house.

FLICK. And those suppers!

[232]

GLICK. And those beds!

SNOW WHITE. No, no! You must stay with me always—always, my brothers.

BLICK. [*Hanging his head.*] But we are—dwarfs.

SNOW WHITE. There are no nobler men in my kingdom! You shall be my bodyguard, and Berthold shall be your Captain.

BLICK. What do you say, brothers?

QUEE. *I* say, Hip, hip, hurrah!

ALL THE DWARFS. Hip, hip, hurrah!

THE WITCH. Dear me! I quite enjoy being respectable! And *I* can't see any reason why you shouldn't live happily ever after.

ROSALYS. Oh Princess, if I don't dance, I shall just die!

CHRISTABEL. And so shall I!

[233]

ALL THE MAIDS OF HONOUR. So shall I! So shall I!

SNOW WHITE. [*To the* PRINCE.] May Queens dance too when they are very, very happy?

THE PRINCE. Do you remember the first words I ever said to you?

> "Lady, may I dance with you
> "In the measure to ensue?"

SNOW WHITE. And I answered;

> "Sir, could any maid withstand
> "Such a flattering command?"
> [*She gives him her hand, and they all whirl*
> *off into the gayest and happiest dance*
> *you can imagine—even the* DWARFS
> *(who, you remember, never could learn)*
> *hopping solemnly for joy, as*

SCENE VII

Music by
Edmond Rickett. Op.25

Vivace (♩.=160)

Piano

ff

Repeat ad lib.

[235]

THE CURTAIN FALLS

P. S.   Snow White and Prince Florimond *did* live happily ever after as the Witch had predicted.

Milton Keynes UK
Ingram Content Group UK Ltd.
UKHW021845180823
427137UK00004B/138